What You Don't Know About Retirement Income Can Hurt You!

Contributing Authors:

Michael Foguth
Shelley Giordano
Will Heil, CPA/PFS, CFP®
Jeff Klauenberg, MA, CIS, CFP®
James B. Merklinghaus
Kyle O'Dell
Jack Tatar
Michael H. Tove, Ph.D., CEP, RFC
Kyle Winkfield

Table of Contents

Tax Efficient Retirement Income

Implications of Healthcare

Using Real Estate for Retirement Income

Introduction: Retirement Income Is the New "Black"

by Jack Tatar

When I began as a financial professional in the nineties, we were called financial consultants. This was a title intended to change the perception that retail financial professionals were not just stock brokers and product pushers, but were actually focused on a client's overall financial situation.

Although I spent most of my time building a business through "cold calling" and placing investors into my preferred investment vehicles, our focus was to go beyond just product to understand our client's full financial needs and situation. Soon financial plans became a standard for clients, and the lower cost options for individual stock trading soon shook out any "old timers" who preferred to be seen strictly as "stock brokers."

Since that time, the industry has changed (for the better, I believe) by having financial advisers (yes, a new title) spend more time on asking clients what their financial goals and objectives are before they recommend any investment options. Today, most financial advisers prefer to utilize money managers for the active management of client portfolios in an effort to position themselves on the "same side of the desk as the client." Advisers are asking more about what a client's dreams for the future are, rather than a focus on who the hot mutual fund manager is these days.

Yes, any financial professional will tell you that the industry has changed over the last twenty years. Most will tell you that that's a good thing and expect even more changes in the future, most with a focus on increasing transparency and improving the overall relationship between client and advisor.

As I've been out of the business of directly advising clients on their financial matters, I've enjoyed watching the trends of the industry over that time. From managed money accounts to lower account fees to alternative investments, I've seen many of the realities of investing and the financial professional change. The truth is that the best financial advisers are those who recognize these changes, embrace them and put them into practice for their clients.

The book that you're now reading was written by these types of financial advisers, professionals and experts who are doing just that. They have their ear to the current realities and demands of the financial marketplace, and are implementing strategies that are focused on helping their clients to navigate these new realities. The authors of this book are not advisers and experts who are remaining in their comfort zone and advising clients on the same tired old investment approaches. They are professionals who understand the current realities of the industry and willing to venture out of their own "comfort zone" to find investment options that are most appropriate for their clients.

With an understanding that every client is different and unique, these professionals recognize that they need to interpret these new realities into customized solutions for each of their clients. When reading this book, it's important to recognize that the solutions presented in these chapters may not be appropriate for all investors and may be very appropriate for others.

The key thing to remember as you read this book, is that if your financial adviser is not discussing these matters with you, you may not have the right adviser. And if your adviser is discussing these items with you, then it's important to work with them and integrate this type of thinking into your financial strategies.

Because the rules and realities of investing have changed, and it's important to have a partner to help you to understand and address these new realities. The advisers and experts in this book recognize the changing landscape and their thinking and level of inquiry is what you should expect of your own financial adviser.

The focus of this book is on a vital aspect of overall financial planning, specifically retirement. We're all aware of the baby boomers and how their reaching retirement age will impact everything from social security to healthcare. It's critical that as people plan for, and enter retirement, no matter what age, they stay current with the realities of what retirement will hold for them. One of these realities is that government has become a major factor in changing the retirement landscape, and there's nothing that can create uncertainty like government. As you read this book, you'll hear the foundations related to retirement moving under your feet as the authors recount how government has change the rules for retirement. Whether its taxes or healthcare, government has taken a "ham handed" approach to changing the rules of retirement that WILL impact many Americans as they reach retirement.

Most of us can remember the ads that we saw that focused on the question of "what's your number?" as a way to create a magical numerical amount that would solve all of your retirement needs. Financial plans were focused on hitting that "number" and the goal to "accumulate" was the primary focus for advisers and clients on their quest to retirement.

However, the realities of retirement have been changing over the last decade. Fewer retirees can depend upon pensions and the income that they provide. Social security considerations for inflation have nearly vanished. A focus on an overall "retirement account value", or "number", along with recent market fluctuations have caused many potential retirees to reconsider their exact retirement date or even if they can retire at all as they watch their "number" take them on a roller coaster ride.

If you've noticed lately, the thinking around retirement has moved away from 'what's my number?' to 'what do I get from that number?'

Investors recognize that planning and saving for retirement will necessitate riding the wave of these fluctuations. With an inability to plan on what the exact number of their retirement nest egg will be, retirees have become more concerned about ensuring a level of income in retirement. They want to know if they can maintain, recreate and protect their current lifestyle in retirement. Many are looking to their retirement accounts not only as a nest egg, but as a way to recreate a paycheck in retirement.

The increased use of annuities by pre-retirees with guaranteed income levels is an example of this trend. Investors have begun flocking to retirement-based annuity products that advertise and market a product's income levels rather than the growth potential of the investment. This trend further shows that the focus for pre-retirees and retirees is now primarily on retirement income, not solely on the size of their retirement account.

This trend has not been lost on investment companies as many more products are being positioned for their income producing benefits. We're also seeing an increased focus by advisors on the income side of a retired or pre-retired client's ledger rather than solely focusing on the asset side (I believe that if you're near retirement and your advisor is not focusing on retirement income and remains solely focused on the growth of your portfolio, you need to begin the discussion or seek other advice).

A friend in the industry said to me the other day that this trend indicates that the financial industry and those planning for retirement now understand that "income is the new black."

As mentioned, this trend has not been lost on the US Government and they're now recognizing that identifying potential retirement income should be the focus for those considering and planning for retirement. This will mean more regulations and changes that you and your adviser need to pay attention to.

An example of this is the Lifetime Income Disclosure Act (https://www.congress.gov/bill/113th-congress/house-bill/2171), which was introduced in 2013 to address this trend and seeks to provide a way for those planning for retirement to gain a handle on what their income will be in retirement, in addition to what their potential asset level will be.

The Department of Labor (DOL), who initiated in 2010 the effort that has resulted in this act, points out that, (http://www.dol.gov/ebsa/newsroom/fsanprm.html)

> *"Workers today face greater responsibility for managing their assets for retirement, both while employed and during their retirement years. This greater responsibility is primarily a result of the trend away from defined benefit plans, where a worker's retirement benefit is typically a specified monthly payment for life, and toward defined contribution plans, where typically contribution, asset allocation and drawdown decisions are made by the participant. Managing finances in order to provide income for life for oneself and one's spouse is a tremendously difficult but important task. Individuals may not understand what savings, asset allocation and drawdown decisions are necessary to achieve both of these goals."*

An effort to address this concern began in 2010 by reaching out to interested parties, including retirement plan providers, investors and financial service firms to understand how best to assist the defined contribution participants with the "important task" of understanding their potential income in retirement. This has led to consideration of a new form of participant disclosure that would require Defined Contribution plan sponsors to display "lifetime income" information on participant benefit statements and thus, impacting the statements of many Americans who are participants in 401k plans.

In 2013, the DOL provided guidance on what this may look like and what would be included on a participant's or beneficiary's benefit statement. Their intent is to provide on the benefit statement the account balance value (as of the last day of the statement period), a projected account balance at retirement, along with lifetime income illustrations.

Now if you're like me, you get a bit skeptical when you hear terms like "projected" values and "illustrations." So let's take a look at what goes into these items.

The "projected" account value is based upon normal retirement age, which means that if a participant has not reached that age (as many 401k participants haven't), according to the DOL brief, the participant's current account balance would be projected to normal retirement age based on assumed future contributions and investment returns. The projected account balance would be converted to an estimated lifetime income stream of payments, assuming that the person retires at normal retirement age.

The DOL goes on to state that the "projections" of account balances are based upon "reasonable assumptions" and Safe Harbor, which are items used by many plans to satisfy fiduciary responsibilities when handling participant investments. The DOL outlines (http://www.dol.gov/ebsa/newsroom/fsanprm.html) this as follows:

When projecting account balances, it is reasonable for a plan administrator to assume:

- *Contributions continue to normal retirement age at the current annual dollar amount, increased at a rate of 3% per year.*

- *Investment returns are 7% per year (nominal).*

- *A discount rate of 3% per year, in order to show the projected account balance in today's dollars.*

In other words, it's "reasonable" to plan for rising investment returns and increased contributions to your plan. Although this may seem optimistic, it still provides some mechanism to evaluate future account balances. Even if we question the integrity of this method, it's probably still better than any that we currently use, if in fact, any of us do have a method.

Let's look at the "income illustration" method. The DOL outlines (http://www.dol.gov/ebsa/newsroom/fsanprm.html) this as well:

When converting current and projected account balances into lifetime income streams, it is reasonable for a plan administrator to assume:

- A rate of interest equal to the 10-year constant maturity Treasury securities rate.

- Mortality as reflected in the applicable mortality table under section 417(e)(3) of the Internal Revenue Code.

- If married, the participant's spouse is the same age as the participant.

- Payments commence immediately and the participant is normal retirement age, if younger than normal retirement age.

To better understand what this all means and potentially could look like, I recommend that you visit the interactive calculator that the DOL has built to compute lifetime income streams in retirement in line with this proposal. It can be found at www.dol.gov/ebsa/regs/lifetimeincome calculator.html

None of this has yet been put into law, and there are of course, those who feel that incorporating this into current plans may create a "hardship" for the providers who will need to integrate this into their systems and reporting mechanisms. With this being said, the reality is that those in the financial services industry are currently moving forward and planning on ways to incorporate income illustrations into the plan reporting for their defined contribution plans.

By the time this makes its way onto participants' statements, I hope that providers and regulators will have effectively worked to simplify what information will be presented and refine the "reasonableness" of the projections used.

The simple fact that the industry and regulators are moving towards this indicates the importance that planning for retirement income is taking for those planning on retirement who contribute and invest in good faith, their hard owned money each paycheck, most with little indication of what they will receive when they finally do retire.

This focus on retirement income rather than a singular focus on "the number", "nest egg" or "account value" is a trend that will require most to plan more effectively for living in retirement.

This trend towards retirement income, or what is also known as "distribution" is the reason that we've gathered these authors together to provide you with a book that outlines these new realities. As you read the chapters, you'll hear the passion and focus that each of these financial professionals have for the wellbeing of their clients.

You'll also note that there may be some differences of opinion between the authors regarding their topics. This is all to remind you that it's critical that you digest this information and work with your own financial adviser to find the right path for retirement income that will work for you. There is not a "magic bullet" for finding a "number" or a distribution strategy that will work for every client.

The important thing is that you become aware of how the rules around retirement income have changed and not being aware of them WILL hurt you!

Allow these authors to help you to understand these new rules so that you can achieve the retirement of your dreams. That should be the focus of every financial adviser working today!

NOTE: A portion of this chapter appeared on the Ally Straight Talk blog at http://community.ally.com/straight-talk/retirement-forget-whats-my-number-whats-my-income/

Section One:
Retirement Accumulation and Distribution

Collecting Income From Your Retirement Savings: A Delicate, Nuanced and Critical Process

Jeff Klauenberg, MA, CIS, CFP®

Retiring or planning on retiring soon? Worries and stress seem to have taken up residence squarely on your chest and are occupying far too many of your thoughts. This was not the retirement playground you had in mind. A trend is developing and the implications of where this evolving course may lead are keeping you up at night.

Here is how the scene is unfolding: in order for your retirement to continue in the style you have chosen, regular withdrawals from your IRA seem to be required. The problem is that if these withdrawals continue, the money will run out long before you had planned. Now you are stuck between a big rock of bills and the hard place of a finite source of retirement capital that is shrinking before your very eyes. The quality of your options is headed in a bad direction.

One of the vital, yet too often overlooked, elements to address as you approach retirement is the evolution of your personal relationship with income. You need to retire your vision of income as a regular stream from an outside source. Your new paradigm is that you have a finite pool of capital, which you have amassed over the years and that must be manipulated in ways that will produce reliable income for the rest of your life.

In more than 30 years in financial planning I have found it common for new retirees to have already devised ways of providing income to help support their chosen lifestyle. Most have a reliable source of steady income: some had Social Security, others a pension, and some have both. Usually this "guaranteed" income does not fully cover lifestyle expenses. Far too often the result is that they dip into their retirement nest egg to make up the difference. Principal is depleted and their ability to produce additional income is hindered. This is what I call, "the withdrawal road to retirement failure."

The most devastating decisions I witness are when a recent retiree decides to withdraw a large lump sum from their IRA to buy a car, remodel the house, or pay off a loan. Many times these withdrawals are made without regard to how the earning power of the original retirement nest egg is reduced forever. Big withdrawals often keep these people from starting retirement with the equivalent power of a 10-cylinder turbo diesel. Instead, they limp along with the earning power of an over-heated 4-cylinder engine trudging uphill in a stiff headwind. They may have new appliances and the car of their dreams, but all of a sudden the road ahead starts looking pretty rough.

Other retirees, while more thoughtful in their approach, are still destined for failure. They establish a plan for systematic withdrawals from retirement funding to fill their income gap. Thinking that their withdrawal routine can mirror the contribution schedule they maintained while earning an income, they unwittingly decimate their retirement earning power by reducing their precious principal. The account that has accumulated all that money over the years is now being treated as an ATM instead of the growth and income powerhouse it could, and should be.

Of course, we reserve an honorable mention for those that have no plan at all. The scenario for these happy-go-lucky few generally ends with considerable time spent greeting strangers entering a department store. Failing to plan is roughly the equivalent of planning to fail, and it is no different for these folks. Be kind and give them a smile on your way into the store. They worked just as hard as you; they just didn't plan as well.

It seems that many of these new retirees are hit with the "I've just won the lottery" syndrome. Prior to retirement, their assets had been firewalled in untouchable accounts maintained by their employer. Contributions came in through regular paycheck deductions, which may have been matched (to some degree) by the employer. The closest the employee ever got to the money was in seeing their monthly or quarterly statement. They never touched the money before retirement.

Upon retirement, their "untouchable" savings and investment plan is handed over to them free and clear. It is now totally open to them. Other than the value of their home, which may be considerable but illiquid, this IRA may be the largest amount of money to which they have ever had access. This account that may be chock full of liquid assets can seem like a treasure chest that just got busted open. In actuality, it's their primary source of wealth that can both grow and produce a regular stream of retirement income. Achieving this is no small feat and requires considerable planning expertise.

All of that ready cash can spawn an unrealistic sense of financial freedom and security. Big-ticket items such as a new kitchen, a new car, a long-awaited vacation, or a one-time payoff of bills now look within their reach. The concept of designing a system that safeguards their principal, creates earnings and delivers a regular income is overshadowed by the gratification of buying the things they have wanted for so long. This is a common scenario and most often does not end well for the retiree that succumbs to the emotionalism of instant rewards at the expense of long-term security.

Messages for New Retirees:

Here are three important concepts that will help you understand how to start a successful retirement:

- The first concept is *Life Expectancy*. Actuarial tables are available on the Internet.[1] Find and review them. As much as you may not

---

1   Try this one from the U.S. Government's Social Security website—http://www.ssa. gov/planners/lifeexpectancy.html

want to think about it, it is vital that you consider the probabilities that apply to the number of years you may yet grace the planet with your presence. Address your own mortality. Consider the implications it has on your retirement savings. Current statistics suggest that you may live until 90 or more.

- The second essential concept is *Matching*. Retirement Income Planning in its simplest form is the matching of your expenses to your retirement income sources and assets. Always be realistic. Always be disciplined

- The third concept is the *Retirement Difference*. Retirees must understand that the pre-retirement life of steady salaries and accumulating assets is *fundamentally* different from their new life of receiving retirement income and withdrawing from retirement assets.

Let's explore each of these important concepts and how each is essential to retirement success.

Life Expectancy

Today you may be thinking that because your parents died before or shortly after retiring, you are destined to do the same. You may be in good health, yet the scenario of dying before being able to enjoy the fruits of your labor guides your retirement thinking. This thinking leads to accumulating things and racking up experiences now. However, while the bucket list gets trimmed down, so does the bank balance. Mickey Mantle famously said, "If I knew I'd live this long, I would have taken better care of myself." For many retirees that did consider their own longevity, the saying might be, "If I knew I'd live this long, I would have taken better care of my money."

With modern healthcare and today's healthier lifestyles, it is becoming more and more common for us to live beyond 90 years. Think about it. If you retire at age 65 and live until age 90, that is a quarter century and a long time for your retirement assets to keep working for you.

I'm reminded here of a good client, Betty B., who was referred to me in 1988. At age 62 she wanted to retire "right now!" because she could start Social Security. Along with her Social Security, she had put aside a decent nest egg. Her reason for retiring "right now" was that she was tired of working and wanted to enjoy the rest of her life. Her parents passed away in their early sixties. Her mother died of a heart attack and her Dad of cancer. Betty was sure that she was destined for the same fate even though she was in good health.

It took some coaching, but I was able to get Betty to extend her outlook for life expectancy a little, and we started on a retirement plan. Each time we met to review her retirement progress and plans, we were able to extend her life expectancy outlook a little longer. Unfortunately she did die one day … at age 89! Through good planning and regular updates of her desires and expectations, she was able to support herself all the way to the end.

You basically have two choices: you can plan to live a short life and end up living "long and poor," or you could plan to live a "long and happy" life and end up having a relaxing and enjoyable retirement.

Matching Expenses to Income and Assets

The only time in life when you did not need an income to cover your expenses was when you were a kid. Remember those years? You probably had it easy, with no worries. Mom and Dad took care of things. Then you grew up.

During your working years you had a salary, or you had net income if you were self-employed. If you were good at managing your expenses, they would match your income. If you purchased something beyond your typical current cash flow, such as a car or home, you borrowed the needed cash. This borrowing was based on your current salary and the expectation of raises in the future. Spending habits were based upon the belief that you would always have new money coming in.

In retirement, you need to match your expenses to your retirement income. This is an altogether different dynamic than what you were accustomed to while working. Be it Social Security, pension, or both, your income is most likely not going to cover all of your needs and wants. Therefore, whatever you have accumulated in, savings, investments and other assets will have to make up the difference. These assets, however large or small, represent a finite pool of money. Managing that money will call for a very specific set of retirement planning disciplines.

Frank and Alice G. come to mind here as a good example. At the time of retirement, they were used to living on $100,000 a year. Once they retired, their combined Social Security equaled $50,000 each year. They also held $800,000 in 401(k) accounts. During their working years, the most they ever had in savings at one time was $30,000.

At retirement, they rolled-over their 401(k) accounts into IRAs. Now they have $800,000 available. The first thing Alice did was to remodel the kitchen to the tune of $20,000. At the same time, Frank was ready to trade in his 100,000 mile daily driver for a new car.

Another $50,000 left the IRA and moved into the garage. He paid cash because he did not want payments.

But wait, there's more. Frank and Alice also got rid of all of their credit card payments and the last student loan, totaling $30,000. They knew that it seemed like a lot of money, but they felt that with $800,000 they should be able to cover the expenses and still be able to comfortably subsist on the remainder. To top it all off Frank and Alice also wanted to start retirement trips that could cost about $8,000 per year.

After all of the spending, Frank and Alice were left with $700,000 at the start of retirement. If they wanted to keep the same lifestyle they had before retiring (requiring $100,000 annually), they would need an extra $50,000 a year from their retirement assets. This meant that they would be withdrawing over 7% each year from their IRAs. To generate that kind of income from their $700,000 base would be very difficult -- and would require a portfolio of high-risk investments. In today's economic environment, where 2% annual return is considered viable for safe investments, 7% is only available with high-risk investments.

If Frank and Alice used a more reasonable withdrawal rate of 4%, they would be able to receive $28,000 a year from their $700,000 remainder. This amount, added to their Social Security, would give them $78,000 per year rather than $100,000. That is a 22% reduction in the annual income they originally were planning. A change in lifestyle was needed, probably starting with eliminating the retirement trips. That was a jagged pill to swallow, but down it went. If they had maintained their $800,000 principal and considered alternate financing and timing for their kitchen, car and debt reduction things would have been different. At the same withdrawal rate of 4% from an $800,000 account, they would have had $32,000 per year in additional income and more choices for how to allocate that income.

Accumulating Assets is Fundamentally Different than Withdrawing Assets

While you were working, you contributed to your retirement plan every pay period. Essentially you were buying shares on a "dollar-cost-averaging" basis. Whether the markets were going up or down, you were adding the same dollar amount.

If you were in the XYZ mutual fund and the share price went up, you bought fewer shares. If the price went down you bought more shares. The fact is, the lower the share price dropped (as in a market crash), the more shares you were buying. When the fund's share price increased, your shares in the fund increased in value. The retirement goal was not how much you had contributed; it was how many shares of XYZ fund you had collected. The more shares you accumulated the more you would have at retirement. As the share price grew, your asset value expanded.

After years of accumulating shares, you retire and now need to sell shares to generate the income you need. Now, if the price of the fund is decreasing, you have to sell more and more shares to realize the same monthly distribution. The more shares you sell, the quicker your portfolio will be depleted. Here is an example:

While working, you contributed $1,000 every month to your IRA (401(k), 403(b)). Each contribution bought you shares in XYZ Fund. Over a six-month period, this is what could happen:

Month	Contribution	Share Price	Number of Shares Bought
1	$1,000.00	$10.00	100
2	$1,000.00	$12.00	83.33
3	$1,000.00	$8.00	125
4	$1,000.00	$7.00	142.86
5	$1,000.00	$9.00	111.11
6	$1,000.00	$10.00	100
Total	**$6,000.00**		**662.30**

As you can see, the higher share price of $12 bought fewer shares while the lower share price of $7 bought more. Although you contributed $6,000 over the six-month period, you were able to buy 662.30 shares of XYZ fund. At the ending share price of $10, you finished with a value of $6,623.00. This is $623.00 more than you invested which is a 10.38% increase in value. While lower share prices due to a decreasing market will lower the overall value of the fund, the drop in share price was a benefit to the number of shares accumulated. A declining share price will always result in buying and accumulating more shares than buying during a flat or increasing market.

You have two basic stages in the life cycle of your retirement savings. Stage one is accumulation when you are depositing money and investing. Stage two is distribution when you are drawing money out at a rate determined by your needs. The real art and science of retirement planning is to expand your accumulated wealth so that assets that both grow and provide income at the same time support you in the years after employment. The three guiding principles in this difficult but achievable endeavor are safety of principal and earnings, consistent growth of assets and adequate income for life.

Let's say you have 20 years to accumulate shares until retirement. At the end of twenty years you start withdrawing money, which requires that you sell shares. You need money to pay your bills. You do not need shares. If you bought shares that were $10 each when you first started buying and were $20 per share by the time you retired twenty years later, you would have an account worth considerably more than the money you put in to it. If the dynamics were reversed and you started buying at $20 and stopped buying at $10, the value of your account would be less than what you deposited. Avoiding this latter scenario requires some particular strategies designed to safeguard your deposits from the risk of loss. Additionally, locking in annual earnings and firewalling them from those same risks are essential.

It can be assumed that over your account's 20-year accumulation period, where the share price goes through periods of rising and lowering price action, the ups and downs will average out. The true problem arises when, in the first few years of retirement, the share price steadily drops. This would cause an increased number of shares to be withdrawn early which would significantly reduced the account's potential for growth and leaves fewer shares available for future withdrawals.

For example, with a static portfolio, (no additions or withdrawals), a 30% loss would require a 43% return over a period of three years to return to where you originally where in value. An account of $100,000 looses $30,000 resulting in a $70,000 balance. The new $70,000 account must increase by the same $30,000, which is 43% of $70,000, to return to the original $100,000 amount. This is possible. But when you are selling shares to take a 4% withdrawal each year for income, you would need a 63% return over three years to get back to even. Your account, because of the combined negative impacts of market losses and withdrawals, will have fallen well below the $70,000 amount in the first example, and would require even more robust returns in order to recover. This is not probable and is the main reason many retirement income plans failed after the market crash of 2008. While all retirement income plans suffered from the bear market drop, newly established withdrawal programs were at a higher risk of depletion, while older plans were more likely to recover.

Sequence of Returns Problem

As shown below, the sequence of positive and negative returns will have little or no effect on a portfolio's value prior to withdrawing.

NO WITHDRAWALS

Year	1	2	3	4	5	6	7	8	9	10	End Balance
$100,000	33.13%	7%	7%	7%	7%	7%	7%	7%	7%	-14%	$196,715
$100,000	-14%	7%	7%	7%	7%	7%	7%	7%	7%	33.13%	$196,715

However, the timing of the negative return can have a significant effect when withdrawing. Using the same scenario and withdrawing 7% ($7,000) income, the negative return in the first year will result in an account value that is $39,515 less.

REGULAR 7% WITHDRAWALS

Year	1	2	3	4	5	6	7	8	9	10	End Balance
$100,000	33.13%	7%	7%	7%	7%	7%	7%	7%	7%	-14%	$110,838
$100,000	-14%	7%	7%	7%	7%	7%	7%	7%	7%	33.13%	$71,323

A Tale of Two Retirees

Here is a story about two similar families that retired four years apart.

Mike and Mary B. retired in January 2004 and Jim and Jane W. retired in January 2008. Mike and Jim worked together, but Mike was four years older. They both started their retirement with IRAs equaling $900,000. They had both been reading retirement articles and books and came to the conclusion that a 4% withdrawal of the initial IRA amount was the optimum rate. This would give them $36,000 a year to supplement their social security.

Mike and Mary enjoyed a strong IRA portfolio performance from 2004 till 2008. Their IRA grew, after the 4% withdrawal, by 6% a year and by the end of 2007 the IRA had a value of $1,204,403. During the Market Crash of 2008 they lost 25%, which included the yearly withdrawal. By April 2009 their IRA's value was $903,302.00, almost what they had started with. Although this hurt quit a lot, they were able to continue their 4% withdrawal program.

Jim and Jane retired 4 years later in January 2008. They felt good about the growth of their IRA and the fact that they had $900,000 to start their retirement. They also read the same material and decided to start a withdrawal program of 4% giving them $36,000 a year. Unfortunately, that first year was not a good one. The Market crashed and between the drop in portfolio value and the withdrawal of $36,000, their portfolio was valued at $675,000 by April 2009. Now they were faced with two decisions. If they continued withdrawing the same $36,000 a year, they would be withdrawing 5.5% of their $675,000, far exceeding the 4% they had determined as safe and reasonable. They were concerned that this rate was too high and their nest egg may run out. If they kept the withdrawal rate at 4%, the new annual withdrawal would be $27,000, a 25% reduction in their income.

That summer of 2009, Mike and Mary were going to take a cruise to Alaska and asked Jim and Jane to join them. Jim and Jane declined. They felt they could not afford it. They needed to stay home and figure out their new retirement plan.

Obviously Mike and Mary retired at the better time. So how do you know when to retire, or start withdrawing an income from your assets? Jim and Jane could not predict the future. So how do you protect your retirement?

Successful Strategies

We have just started to scratch the surface of the many factors that influence the strategic planning that underpins the funding your retirement lifestyle. The dynamics of your money management change dramatically once you retire. Drawing down your wealth, providing a significant and reliable income, while keeping your assets growing productively yet safely is a nuanced undertaking. Regular contributions to your retirement savings are a vital practice that must be adhered to religiously. Safeguarding your accumulated wealth is a priority, as is locking your annual earnings and protecting the entire amount from undue risk. Once you enter the distribution phase and start withdrawing assets from your retirement account in order to provide your retirement income, a whole new set of risks arise. Maintaining an awareness of the status of your accounts, developing a solid and realistic distribution plan and adjusting your expectations according to market and personal changes will contribute to a higher quality retirement for you and your family.

Increasing Income from Decreasing Assets

By: Michael Foguth

This Is Not Your Grandfather's Retirement

The dynamics of retirement planning are changing rapidly, as are many other aspects of life in the 21st century. The popular post-war American arrangement of long-term employment with a single company resulting in a home, cars, Social Security, a pension, health and death benefits and possibly even a couple of worthwhile investments is as out of place today as Spielberg's dinosaurs on the local playground. This is not your grandfather's retirement scenario anymore. Relative to the halcyon days of generations passed, you are now pretty much on your own.

It is incumbent on you to plan for your retirement.

Here is one interesting way to look at it: if you are lucky, you will arrive at a point in your life when you depart the ranks of the employed and live the rest of your days with a regular, stable and sufficient income fueled by assets which reduce at a pace that assures you will never outlive your money. How does somebody successfully plan to pay him or herself a steady paycheck for possibly twenty years or more with a pile of assets that are continually shrinking because they are being drawn down to supply the river of paychecks?

Potential Bumps In The Road

Don't forget that inflation can jump up and take a bite out of your plan any old time it pleases. While inflation has been low for a few years, it is always ready to start a run uphill as the economy improves. Then there are cost-of-living adjustments. Are they the same as inflation, or based on inflation? While we are asking questions pertinent to your retirement, how about this one: how long are you going to live? How many years are your resources going to need to last?

Since 1975 Social Security's benefit increases have been based on a general calculation of change in the cost of living from one year to the next. Since inflation has been relatively tame for the past few years, the COLA (cost of living adjustment) for 2015 will be an increase of just 1.7% over 2014 benefit levels. Projections of COLA figures are important for your retirement planning. The earlier in your career that you initiate your planning, the more impact the COLA numbers are likely to have as the effects of the increases will compound over time.

To make matters even a bit more challenging, consider that interest rates have remained at or near historic lows for an extended period. This can be great if you are looking to buy real estate or other major assets that can involve borrowing money. A 30-year mortgage at 3% can be pretty attractive compared to the 10% days of the nineties.

On the other hand, if you are using money as a tool to accumulate more money for retirement, low interest rates can slow your progress. A Certificate of Deposit purchased in 2007, when the rate of return was over 5%, was only returning close to 1% by 2012. On a $1 million principal amount, the difference in annual return is around forty thousand dollars. For someone basing his or her retirement plan on the growth of this asset, that disparity can be profound.

Add to this gumbo of issues affecting your retirement planning the ever-popular subject of taxes. A common mistake for retirees in mapping out their financial future is miscalculating the bite that taxes will take out of their retirement income. How you invest, withdraw, spend or otherwise utilize your assets can make a difference in the treatment of your income by state and federal governments. Sometimes unexpected tax payments can be the difference between going on vacation and staying home. It may even mean the difference between self-sufficiency and dependence.

Let's say that your expectations for retirement income do not include allowance for annual increases due to cost-of-living adjustments. When your Social Security benefits are greater than you anticipated, you might feel gratified that you are getting more than you bargained for. The problem is that your increased income could drive you into a higher tax bracket and the increase in taxes owed could create a deficit that exceeds the increase in income. While this is not a circumstance experienced by many retirees, it does happen and it highlights the need for detailed and informed planning from the outset of your retirement considerations.

Defense Wins Championships

After a lifetime of toil, trouble and saving here comes the end of the days of gainful employment. There is a light at the end of the tunnel. Is it the shimmer of glorious fun and relaxation, or is it a gorilla with a flashlight? It all depends on how much quality planning you have in place as you near the end of the employment tunnel.

Along with the obstacles to maximizing your retirement income discussed earlier, there are plenty of other opportunities for your assets to be depleted and for your plans or lifestyle to be negatively impacted. These things can vary from changes in the tax laws to a catastrophic accident or illness. Perhaps a family member requires assistance and you decide to step in and offer a loan or gift. Let's take a look at some effective ways to defend your assets from contingencies and threats that lie in wait out there in the retirement finance jungle.

Keep Your Eye On The Prize

The goal we are addressing here is to keep your retirement income stream consistent even as your assets are decreasing because you are using them up. We have covered some of the basic dynamics at play in this process. Now, let's get specific about the menu of tools at your disposal for hitting your target.

It's now time to define your objective. You have to figure out how much retirement income you will require and for how long you are likely to need it. To arrive at these estimates, you are going to reverse engineer your retirement income scenario.

The first step in this process is to calculate your probable life expectancy. Your family health history, personal health and social history along with various other stressors and influences all have bearing on the actuarial projections of your life span. As this can be a difficult batch of information to digest (after all, you are studying your own mortality), lean on your advisor for appropriate surveys and other tools to make certain that all necessary information is considered.

One important thing to keep in mind is that we are all living longer and racking up bigger health expenses than ever before. Our prolonged lifespan is extended into that portion of our time where we are most vulnerable to malady and old age. Selecting a thorough survey and well-respected actuarial formulas are crucial in this exercise. These are devices with which your advisor should be intimately familiar.

Once you have a realistic time window for the duration of your retirement, then you move on to your budget. Questions of lifestyle, activities, heirs, gifts and other allocations are all tallied up to construct your retirement budget. Again, your advisor should have deep resources to help you dig deep and make certain that you are considering all the angles. From trips to helping family with education or other needs to taxes and other expenses, it is hard to over-stress the need for accuracy and thoroughness in developing your retirement budget.

With a timeframe and income needs identified, you can start earmarking some potential products that will help you utilize your retirement assets to manufacture that steady stream of income. The challenge from this point is how to find the right instruments that will safely utilize your savings to meet your retirement income needs while maintaining some buffer of assets for contingencies and emergencies as discussed above. Again, defending the castle against inflation, market fluctuations, a long retirement and taxes is job one. You are looking for the right product that will not risk your principal, will allow you to secure annual earnings and will provide a dependable adequate income stream.

Often these parameters will pretty much narrow the field to annuities and a few other life insurance products. Deciphering the esoterics of these products can be daunting. Not only are there many types of each, but also the interactions of these products with each other, the costs of these different products, and the effective blending of these instruments with other assets and investments as well with your tax planning require a deft hand. Deciding if they're right for you is not an easy decision and not something to make on your own, or without doing thorough research.

Choose Your Vehicles Wisely

There are many types of financial tools and instruments that can help you protect your capital while generating dependable retirement income. We are going to look at annuities and examine how this unique type of insurance product can provide safety for your capital while delivering a guaranteed income stream for a specified time span. Coming in a wide variety of flavors, an annuity is an insurance product that can offer safety, security and tax-advantages. Similar to Qualified Plans such as a 401(k) or an IRA, money invested in an annuity is allowed to grow on a tax-deferred basis; it can grow without being taxed, but the earnings will be taxed when distributed to the annuity holder.

When you purchase an annuity, normally from an insurance company, your money is invested in underlying securities at the discretion of the insurance company. In return you collect interest, your principal and earnings grow without being subjected to taxation (yet) and you will receive payments according to a schedule that you and the issuer agree to at the time of purchase. Unlike qualified plan accounts like a 401(k) or an IRA, there is no limit to the amount that can be invested in an annuity.

It can be more than daunting to try and select the right annuity once you start to examine the field of options. This is where your retirement planner can really make a serious contribution to the cause. How you structure your assets, how and when you receive income, how much income you get and on what schedule as well as other factors can all play into your tax strategy.

All of these issues point to the fact that your retirement income level is not merely a function of the quantity or type of assets you have accumulated, it is also highly dependent on how those assets are positioned, utilized and coordinated at the time of and during your retirement.

Narrow the Field

We're going to focus on annuities, as they can potentially address your need for both protection and income production. An annuity is a life insurance product that offers protective features for firewalling your capital from unnecessary risk as well as design features that can provide for long-term payments to you. In some cases, they can help you achieve certain tax advantages, depending upon a variety of factors. Most of all, an annuity meets your retirement planning objectives of asset safety and income security.

To specifically address these challenges of growing your assets pre-retirement, providing a secure regular income during retirement as well as guaranteeing that your assets last as long as you do, we are going to examine the Fixed Index Annuity (FIA). A fixed annuity is like a bank CD in that it earns interest on your investment while shielding your investment and earnings from unwanted market risks. In addition to these earnings and safety features, a fixed annuity guarantees a payout (the fixed part) according to a schedule agreed upon by the buyer and insurance company at the time the annuity is purchased.

The Index component refers to the earnings function of the annuity. An FIA calculates earnings according to the performance of a selected financial market index, such as the Dow Industrials and S&P500. The advantage here is that you have the opportunity to annually lock in index gains on a tax-deferred basis. This gives you the safety of a CD complemented by a capacity to participate in market upswings while limiting your exposure to downturns.

When the safety and earnings features are combined with the guaranteed payout schedule, you have a powerful tool for meeting your retirement needs. Within this framework, it is important to understand that a number of factors that can influence the price, performance and payouts of your annuity. For instance, your annuity may be purchased with pre-tax dollars. The result being that your entire payout will be taxable at the time it is delivered to you.

Questions you'll need to ask are: Will the payment amount to the insurance company have any impact on your tax rate calculation at the time of your purchase? Will the payout amount be enough to drive you into a higher tax bracket in your retirement? What are the potential impacts, if any, in both cases? You may want an analysis of both scenarios, purchasing with pre-tax and after-tax dollars.

Surrender periods, which are part of your annuity contract with the issuing financial institution, are something you and your advisor will also need to consider. During the surrender period you agree to keep the majority of your annuity investment in the contract. In general, you will find that surrender periods last from five to ten years. Often, an annuity contract will allow you to make withdrawals of as much as 10% per year of the accumulated value without penalty. However, if you withdraw more than 10%, you will pay a surcharge on everything above the 10% level. Surcharge amounts vary, but are usually between 5% and 10%. Often, the surcharge amount is on a sliding scale and reduces to zero by the end of the surcharge period.

Here's the Rub

Looking ahead, it becomes clear that some seemingly unrelated forces are actually aligning to combine with each other to produce some negative effects on your prospects for a financially secure retirement. Let me explain.

Inflation is pretty tame these days, staying below 3% per year. At the same time, for men and women that are currently 65 years old, their chances of surviving until 90 are about one in three. These longevity figures have never been so high or so favorable. Relatively low inflation and favorable longevity numbers, it all looks pretty rosy, right?

Let's take a closer look. If you are living on $50,000 per year, in 25 years you will need $104,689 annually to maintain exactly the same style of life with just a 3% inflation rate. Remember buying a gallon of milk in 1990? It cost you around $1.50. That same gallon runs you about $3.90 today. If inflation should start to climb above 3%, the situation just gets worse.

How in the world do you defend against this ballooning cost-of-living expense that is exacerbated by the probability that you are going to survive a good long while? Returning to the Fixed Income Annuity that we highlighted earlier, we find some convenient solutions to this common but mostly overlooked problem.

Here is how it works; let's say you deposit some of your retirement savings into this FIA account and in 5 or 10 years you need income to start paying you every month. The starting income will be set at a percentage based on your age, this becomes the starting value of your income, and every year your starting income value will increase based on a fixed rate or an indexed rate that you and your financial professional can select.

The rate you choose will be based either on reasonable projections of the probable inflation rate increases or to another external guide such as the Social Security COLA or perhaps a market index. It is up to you and your advisor to make the selection that best suits your sensibility and circumstance. The long-term value of this account is based on the fact that you can never have less income than the previous year, it will only increase from the previous year. Even if you live into your 90's and have spent all of your original deposit plus the interest you have earned over the years, your annual income will still increase from the previous year.

Like most insurance products, the issuer bases their participation on the probabilities amalgamated from the actuarial projections regarding large pools of customers. Whether or not your particular contract is one that makes or loses money for them is not the point. Their interest is in the fact that from the entire universe of contracts that they have issued, they will profit. Should you outlive your contributions and earnings from your contract, more power to you. Regardless of the number of years that you enjoy retirement, you have an income that guarantees that cost-of-living increases will not devalue your income stream nor force you to lower the standards of your chosen retirement lifestyle.

Good Intel Means Good Outcomes

These are just some of the many factors at play with the purchase of these complex financial instruments. If you have been thorough and honest in the process of informing your lifespan expectations and retirement budget calculations, you should have a pretty accurate picture of your retirement needs. Use this as your guide. Virtually every instrument that you can employ in order to safely manage your retirement assets will have a complex series of issues that you and your advisor must consider. When you are certain of your needs, desires and resources it makes coping with the selection of instruments and dealing with the underlying intricacies much easier.

One of the mysteries of retirement planning is the creation of a secure and stable flow of income from a collection of assets that are getting smaller due to the fact that they are the source of the income. We have uncovered some of the possibilities with FIAs here, and, perhaps more importantly, exposed the possibility that you can achieve this goal of providing a steady stream of income to meet your retirement budget needs utilizing a decreasing pool of assets.

The universe of choices for products to meet your retirement needs is not only large and growing, but it is constantly changing. Annuities have remained a solid choice for generations and look to remain so. Still, the swirl of taxation, longevity, inflation, legislation and product alteration issues presents an education challenge even for the most studied professional. Your most valuable asset when selecting the best instruments for your retirement needs is quality information. Supply yourself and your planner with the most accurate details you can regarding your accumulation of retirement-dedicated assets, the expected duration of your retirement based on your life expectancy and your financial needs during retirement. This is your greatest assurance that you will end up with a properly configured and calibrated retirement income with which you can feel secure.

Section Two:
Creating Lifetime Income

Lifetime Assurances Are Possible

By James B. Merklinghaus

One of the biggest concerns new clients come to me with is fear of outliving their money. In two separate studies, one by Allianz[2] and the other by Wells Fargo,[3] people said they feared running out of money more than death. The sad truth is, their worst fears will come true unless they take proactive steps to avoid that from happening.

The retirement crisis in America is real; almost half of Americans ages 25 to 64 are on track to retire near poverty and will have no money to live on other than social security, according to a study released by the Schwartz Center for Economic Policy Analysis at the New School.[4] Ask anyone crunching household budget numbers, and it's clear Social Security can't come close to replacing income in retirement for most Americans, especially with the changes in Medicare.[5]

The anxiety is real, and it's from fear of the unknown. More than 30% of study respondents said they weren't sure what their retirement expenses would be.[6] That's true of many of my new clients that first walk through my door. They have no idea what their expenses will be, or even

---

2   http://www.aarp.org/work/retirement-planning/info-06-2010/running_out_of_money_worse_than_death.html

3   http://time.com/money/3581647/retirement-savings-outlive-death-worse/

4   http://www.economicpolicyresearch.org/images/docs/research/retirement_security/Are_US_Workers_Ready_for_Retirement.pdf

5   http://www.medicare.gov/your-medicare-costs/costs-at-a-glance/costs-at-glance.html

6   http://www.economicpolicyresearch.org/images/docs/research/retirement_security/Are_US_Workers_Ready_for_Retirement.pdf

when they want to retire. Typically, the only savings they have is in the form of funds accumulated in employer-sponsored retirement plans such as 401(k)s. And more often than not, these accounts are worth less than what they had anticipated when they first started out.

The 401(k) experiment has failed a lot of people, and many have seen their savings disappear with the stock debacles of 2000 and 2008. The 401(k) was never meant to be a mainstream pension plan. According to the Urban Institute, retirement accounts lost 32% of their value between September 2007 and December 2008.[7] The Institute further indicated that while economic downturns can impede retirement goals, research has found laddering annuities can be an effective strategy in many market conditions.[8]

What is Laddering?

Laddering is more commonly associated with CDs and bonds, but laddering annuities is a very effective strategy to cure that fear of outliving your retirement assets. Laddering annuities effectively comes down to the skill of the person devising the strategy, the insurance companies and the available riders.

Annuities are state-regulated and only licensed life insurance companies are authorized to issue them. Each annuity an insurer wants to promote must meet standards set by the state Department of Insurance.

My firm ladders annuities and riders from a handful of insurance companies whose annuity products meet a strict set of guidelines. There are a few ways to approach a laddering strategy, but the main idea is investing in annuities that begin and end at different times. We ladder based upon the time of purchase of the annuities, as well as the time of payout, or target multiple payout periods.

Done right, there will be diversification and income payout, even guaranteeing clients that they won't outlive their source of income in retirement. That's the main goal to keep in mind with annuities—it's

---

7   http://www.urban.org/search?search_api_views_fulltext=retirement
8   http://www.urban.org/search?search_api_views_fulltext=retirement

about the lifetime income. Every client has different needs and concerns, and each requires a specialized solution to meet individual goals.

Why a 401(k) Can't Replace a Pension

Jeff and Sandra came to me in a panic. After barely rebounding from the 2008 hits on their 401(k)s, they still ignored my advice, keeping all their eggs in one volatile basket. Now well in their 60s, they always felt they had plenty of time to save, and between kids in college, the house, new computer, etc., there was never time to worry about retirement. Besides, they had Sandra's hefty pension.

"The company closed, overnight. Bankrupt. No warning," Sandra sobbed. "No one knows what will become of our pensions, if they're even safe. No one knows anything!"

With pensions, the employer invests the assets and guarantees the money, while the worker takes home reduced earnings. Then, when retirement comes, the pension delivers a certain percentage of pay based on years of service until the worker dies. Sandra, having been with the company well over 30 years, was entitled to a nice pension, which was something the couple was counting on.

In contrast, defined contribution plans, such as 401(k)s, allows employees to set aside tax-deferred income for retirement purposes. With a 401(k), there's no guarantee of income, something Sandra and Jeff saw many times over the years with market fluctuations.

Not only were they dealing with the sudden loss of income, they were worried about the possibility of losing the only real retirement vehicle they had in place—Sandra's pension. While I assured them the pension would likely work out, that even in bankruptcy most employees see most or all of their pension money, the real job was to start retirement planning with long term security in mind.

Laddering for Lifetime Guarantees

Sandra and Jeff got a scare that made them take a look at all their assets and forced them to set some hard goals about the future and when they wanted to retire—and how they wanted to live. In order to achieve their goals, they wanted guarantees they wouldn't outlive their money. The thought of living on public assistance, or with family was out of the question, they said. Sandra's job scare set them straight and they got their financial house in order. I'm happy to report that Sandra did get her pension, and within a year's time they decided to downsize and retire with lifetime income in mind.

My laddering strategy using annuities gave Sandra and Jeff a guaranteed income stream so they wouldn't have to rely on Sandra's pension or their social security. When an investment is laddered, units are deliberately purchased at different times or with different maturities, and are measured by risk or time period.

There are many vehicles to consider when laddering but if you want guarantees—and money to last a lifetime—I always use annuities. My custom strategy uses insurance companies that have been in operation for over 100 years and never accepted government TARP funds. It's a unique set of companies offering certain contracts and income riders. Any good laddering system should be flexible enough to meet unexpected changing requirements of any client's situation during retirement years.

What are Annuities?

An annuity is nothing more than a contract between you and an insurance company. In exchange for a lump-sum investment or series of investments, you are provided with a reliable income stream for a certain period of time. There are three main types of annuities, each serving a different purpose.

Fixed Annuities offer a guaranteed rate of return based on current interest rates and periodic payments in a fixed amount. The longer the payments are scheduled to last, the less the payment amount will be.

Indexed Annuities offers a higher return, typically based on the S&P 500, but capped at no more than 8%. They are guaranteed a minimum contract value, regardless of index performance.

Variable Annuities offers the option of investing in the market (usually mutual funds). Return is based on how your investments perform, and just as your rate of return varies, your income will as well.

All annuities are classified as either qualified or nonqualified annuities. *Nonqualified annuities* are purchased with after-tax money, funds that already have been taxed by the IRS. An example would be your take home pay (the amount on your paycheck that's payable to you), those are your after-tax funds (barring other deductions you might have, like health or life insurance).

If you saved money from your paychecks and purchased a nonqualified annuity, only the interest earnings would be taxable as ordinary income when it came time to take your distribution.

Qualified annuities are purchased with before tax dollars, a common scenario being when you're rolling money from an IRA or 401(k). The contribution itself could qualify for a tax deduction, but when you take the distribution, the entire amount is subject to ordinary income taxes.

The rules and ideas behind qualified versus nonqualified are defined by the tax code, not the insurance companies or brokers.

Are Annuities for Everyone?

Robert C. Merton, the 1997 Nobel Prize winner in Economics, said in the Harvard Business Review that he thinks annuities should be used as a primary retirement vehicle.[9] Anti-401(k), he says the average person planning retirement should be thinking in terms of buying a future income stream, not choosing funds they know nothing about. He says people shouldn't be asked about their level of risk-averseness, they should be asked at what age they want to retire and with how much income.

I agree with the famed economist. It's actually two of the top three questions I ask my retirement clients: When do you want to retire? How much income do you need? When will you need this money? You don't

---

9   https://hbr.org/2014/07/the-crisis-in-retirement-planning

buy an annuity if you're saving for a down payment on a house in a few years. An annuity isn't for you if you'll need the money for college soon.

An annuity is an investment vehicle used to convert current wealth into a later income stream. It's the only retirement instrument I recommend when clients want an income stream and no "maybes" when it comes to payout. When annuities are setup correctly, your income stream will actually increase in retirement, but you'll never risk losing a penny. Annuities are the only transfer of risk strategy that guarantees an income stream you—and your spouse if applicable—can never outlive. Even if you draw the annuity account to zero because you lived too long, you still get a monthly check until you die. If the annuity is setup correctly, that monthly check goes to your significant other until death.

An income rider is a benefit you can add to an annuity that is the same as giving yourself—and your partner—a pension. Income riders provide you with a guaranteed income for life without having to give up access to remaining principal. You get a guaranteed rate of return, are protected from investment risk, and any fees can be charged to the balance left for your heirs, thereby never affecting your monthly income.

Penalties, fees and downsides

The major downside to an annuity is that it's not a high growth product, and there is no liquidity. You're also locking in current interest rates, which is why laddering for lifetime income is often a good strategy to combat low rates.

You withdraw your money early, but it will cost you. Simply put, as soon as the annuity is issued, 87.5% is available if you had to immediately surrender it in the event of an emergency. Surrender charges are not much different than the early withdrawal penalties you pay if you cash in early on other investment vehicles. If you need to cash in your annuity early, there are surrender charges, taxes plus additional penalties if you withdraw before age 59.5. There are some annuities with up-front fees, but they're not products I personally use. Asking the right questions before you buy an annuity is key.

There are fees associated with income riders, but it's usually less than 1.25% and can be structured to be tacked on to your heir's inheritance, and not affect your monthly check. Again, asking the right questions is paramount to avoid any surprises. When income riders are added to an annuity, you and your partner are guaranteed money coming in for life. Even if you draw the account to zero, you'll receive a check every month until the day you and your partner pass away. If there's money left, it goes to your heirs. You can't do that with any other type of investment instrument.

Avoiding Tax Traps

I'm a big fan of nonqualified annuities with an exclusion ratio, and Jeff and Sandra are now too. The only product that can have an exclusion ratio is a nonqualified annuity issued by an insurance company. The laddering system I setup for them using this type of annuity, gave them a contractual guarantee that they will not outlive their money. Nonqualified annuities using the lifetime income option create the benefit of an exclusion ratio.

The lifetime income option provides Jeff and Sandra with monthly money for the rest of their lives that neither can outlive. For example, one piece of their investment strategy is a $100,000 nonqualified annuity with an exclusion ratio that will give them $700 in monthly income. No matter how long they live, their payments continue. In other investments, once the account is exhausted, payments stop.

The exclusion ratio is the percentage of the annuity payment that is classified as nontaxable income. It's calculated by dividing the after-tax money used to buy the annuity, by the life expectancy of the person receiving the payments. The actual exclusion ratio is provided by the insurance company and is based on a number of factors, including IRS law and actuary tables.

The exclusion ratio is a unique method used only by insurance companies to calculate a monthly payment when a large percentage of that payment is tax-free and just a small portion is taxable. This is achieved by using the client's mortality based on the age they are when they decide to turn on income.

The older a person is when the annuity is started, the greater the exclusion ratio will be, possibly providing for significant tax-free income. Tax obligation on the interest earned is then spread over that span of time. Otherwise the interest is taxable in the year you take the money. With nonqualified annuities with an exclusion ratio,

- Your principle is guaranteed
- Any interest gained is protected if the market fails to provide returns
- You'll generate monthly income that has favorable tax treatment
- You'll never outlive your money

The interest from this annuity is taxed as ordinary income, but the principal is tax-free because it's a return of your initial investment. The IRS considers 70% to 75% of the money you withdraw as a return of principal, so only 25% to 30% is taxable.[10] The amount of principal returned in each payment is determined by the same factors used to calculate how much income you'll receive; it assumes that the principal will be returned to you equally over the payout period.

For example, if Jeff and Sandra start using their annuity for living expenses at $700 a month but didn't take the lifetime income option, all of their interest that was deferred would be subject to immediate taxation. Simply put, interest building in an annuity is deferred until the money is used. Without the lifetime income option, a larger portion of the funds are immediately treated as interest and subject to taxation the year they're withdrawn.

The same $700 with a lifetime income option, a larger portion is treated as principal and a much smaller part is interest. Therefore, you'll pay taxes just on the interest income. All other payouts are considered principal and aren't subject to federal or state taxes.

---

10 http://www.irs.gov/publications/p554/ch02.html

Jackie's Tax Scenario

Jackie just retired at 69, and she knows she wants lifetime income from her $200,000 retirement savings. The IRS tables indicate her lifetime will be 18 more years, or 87 years old.[11]

Investment Amount	$200,000
Payout Period	18 years
Annual Payment	$15,288
Total Payments Over Life Expectancy	$275,184
Exclusion Ratio	72.6%

That means that $11,099 of each annual payment is a tax-free return of principal, which leaves $4,188 as taxable income. Payments received after 18 years will be fully taxable because there is no more principal to return.

The amount of income is based on prevailing long-term interest rates and how old you are at the time you set up the annuity. The older you are when the annuity is set to begin, the higher the income, since according to calculations, you'll have fewer years to live. But, it's possible to include your spouse so that the income is paid as long as one of you is alive. This is accomplished by way of an annuity contract provided by the insurance company. The monthly payment is slightly smaller while you're both alive, but you'll both get checks until death.

Jackie was predeceased by her husband and her children were left an inheritance then. Her biggest concern was remaining independent and not outliving her money. Social security and a pension covered most of her bills, so she was in a perfect position for a laddering strategy.

Her interest rate is guaranteed never to go down and she will never outlive her money. Further, her principal is guaranteed too, and she'll

---

11 http://www.irs.gov/publications/p590b/

generate income with tax benefits. That's what laddering nonqualified annuities with an exclusion ratio can do, provided it's done correctly.

Payments are determined when the income stream is turned on, and is primarily based on your life expectancy at that time. Different ages and gender will create different payments.

It's About Income and Time

It's actually quite easy to get lifetime assurances, and it doesn't take much more than a little planning and a shift of expectations. Laddering annuities is about generating income for life—not doubling your money in 30 days. People should not fear outliving their money. With the right strategy, no one will ever have to.

The amount people should invest in a lifetime income option account, be it laddered or otherwise, comes down to spending needs. The payout should be enough to cover your projected monthly living expenses.

Laddering "produces more guaranteed lifetime income, develops more liquidity to address other retirement needs and builds more long-term wealth than other commonly adopted retirement income strategies," according to a report by Mass Mutual.[12] In an article in Investopedia, the report found that strategies involving income annuities outperformed the strategy of having stock and bonds only, regardless of market conditions.[13]

Your portfolio is never really put to the test until you're officially ready to retire. What if you're ready and the stock market isn't? Remember, you're constantly adding to your retirement account during your working years. The day you retire, you'll only have withdrawals, no more deposits.

It never occurs to people that they're going to be in the market for 40 years or better, and then in retirement just as long. If everyone used an investment vehicle in just part of their portfolio that guaranteed their

---

12 http://www.investopedia.com/articles/retirement/09/laddering-annuities. asp#ixzz3gYI3jUPO

13 http://www.investopedia.com/articles/retirement/09/laddering-annuities. asp#ixzz3gYI3jUPO

principal against market loss, that would account for at least 12 years of guaranteed retirement income. If you want to retire at 70 and plan for 30 years of income, at least you'll have 12 years of guaranteed principal waiting for you. That's a start.

The first advice I give new clients is to live within your means. Nothing beats the natural laws of investment: put a small amount of money away over a long period of time. There is no get rich quick scheme in retirement. You're much better off having guarantees that deposit money directly into your account on a systematic basis with no chance of fluctuation. There are now income riders that allow for actual income increase during retirement payouts, which can't be reduced during market downturns.

Questions to ask

Before buying an annuity or income rider, there are some questions you should ask yourself and your investment professional.

Conclusion

Many people aren't aware that there is another safe investment choice besides banks, and that's insurance companies. There is no better assurance when it comes to safe places to grow your money long term than high quality , reputable insurance companies.

Let's think about the safe haven people consider banks. A bank will take 10% of your deposit and keep it safe with a like investment from its assets, while the other 90% is loaned out by the board of directors to the investments of their choice. If a bank goes under, you get an application to fill out to get your money, and you may not get interest during the waiting time, which is allowed to take up to 30 years.

Insurance companies offer much greater assurance. Clients are always able to get their money. The better insurance companies have a $1.60 to $2.10 retention ratio on every dollar you have invested with them. The insurance companies pay into state guarantee funds, which protects you if an individual company defaults. Even if a company defaults, the policyholder continues to receive its regular payments. Eventually the insurance company's assets are settled through the bankruptcy courts and another insurance company will buy the rights to the policyholders. The policyholders will then be offered an equivalent policy or the chance to move forward with their balance.

Markets, Required Minimum Distributions, and the 4% Rule

Michael H. Tove Ph.D., CEP, RFC

We spend our lives saving for retirement. Financial advisors are very skilled at telling clients how to invest. Whether or not those investments perform according to expectations is another matter. But, when it comes to converting the retirement savings into retirement income, the details of that advice often becomes muddy. Fundamentally, most advisors know a lot more about building an investment portfolio than how to effectively convert it into permanent lifetime income when it is needed.

Central to understanding this is to recognize that the investing cycle has two active and diametrically opposed phases: The first phase is "Accumulation" where contributions (amount other than investment return) are made to a future account. These contributions may be direct (personal contributions from earned income or inheritance) and indirect (third parties like an employer). The second phase is "Decumulation" where that account is used to generate future income; in other words, spent.

Robert C. Merton (2014), Nobel laureate and distinguished professor of finance at the MIT Sloan School of Management and Professor Emeritus at Harvard University, and others (e.g., Marcks and Kalamarides 2011) have strongly criticized corporate America for their abandonment of Defined Benefit Plans, commonly known as Pensions, in exchange for Defined Contribution Plans like the 401(k). Where Defined Benefit Plans guarantee a specific income for life, Defined Contribution Plans merely specify how much the employer and employee may contribute each month, and "trust" the stock market to do the rest. In other words, it was a shift from "we'll take care of you for life" to a "good luck in your retirement!" Their central message is that when it comes to retirement planning, people *need to think about monthly income, not net worth.*

Marcks and Kalamarides, citing data by Prudential Financial, reported that "only 13% of individuals say they are "very confident" they'll have enough money" in retirement. In other words, the vast majority of investors are NOT "very confident" about the reliability of their retirement investment plans. Their anxiety and frustration lies in lack of viable alternatives offered because the sins of corporate America are no worse than what personal investment advisors tell their clients. Those advisors want you to believe—because *they* believe, that markets are sufficiently reliable for long-term income generation. This belief stems from a concept known as the "4% Rule."

First proposed by William Bengen (1994), the 4% Rule was a derivation of popular thought from Peter Lynch (and others) that investors could live off 7% of their investment assets annually and never outlive their money. These ideas, as seemingly attractive as they were, soon caught criticism from a number of economists who opined that markets could not be expected to always rise at 7.53% per year, the amount of increase necessary to offset a 7.0 withdrawal (losses impact a portfolio disproportionally more than gains).

Bengen proposed that, using a conservative model of 50% stocks and 50% bonds, an investor could generate permanent lifetime income by withdrawing 4% off an investment portfolio every year and rely on market growth to replenish the amount paid out. The plan continued further to recommend a 3% annual increase in payments to keep pace with inflation. In 1998 (the "Trinity Study"), Cooley, Hubbard and Waltz reaffirmed Bengen's model. Later, Bengen (2006) updated his recommendations to suggest that if the money was received tax-free, the safe withdrawal rate increased to 4.5% and if taxable, 4.1%.

However, Bengen's conclusions were derived during latter half of the 20th Century, a time characterized by very stable market conditions. In fact, from the end of World War II (and the "official" end to the great depression) through the mid-1990s (when Bengen first published), U.S. Markets had experienced only one major upset. On October 19, 1987 ("Black Monday") the Dow Jones Industrial Average® dropped 22.61%, the biggest one-day market crash in U.S. history. At the time, it seemed to recall the 1929 crash that precipitated the Great Depression. But by August 1, 1989, less than two years later, it had fully recovered and the long-term impact of that crash to the average investor was minimal.

Then starting January 3, 1995 markets took off on what would become the greatest Bull Market run in U.S. history. Through March 24, 2000, the S&P 500 Index® roared upward at an enviable average rate of 21.21% per year. It made thousands of otherwise unsophisticated investors, especially those in high tech markets, into overnight millionaires. With everyone intoxicated by the glory of phenomenal newfound wealth, few were wondering about long-term sustainability. But almost from the start, there were warning signs that the good times would not last.

In 1996, Sterling Professor of Economics at Yale and future Nobel Laureate, Robert J. Shiller, in a briefing to the Fed, characterized the markets as behaving with "Irrational Exuberance" (2000, 2005). Shortly after, on December 5, 1996, Fed Chair Alan Greenspan used Shiller's term in a speech at the American Enterprise Institute. Based on those two words, world markets plunged from 2.3% to 4.0%. Although they quickly recovered, it was a harbinger of things to come.

In 1999, the world became increasingly alarmed about what would happen to computers at the stroke of midnight on January 1, 2000. Called "Y2K," the problem was that calendar year data was programmed as only two digits (e.g. "99" referred to "1999"). The concern was that in 2000, "00" would be misread as "1900." Rampant predictions of calamity generated a huge demand for upgrading computing systems.

In response to that demand, came an unprecedented onslaught of high tech entrepreneurs offering IPOs on every imaginable new computing company. Many of those start-up "Dot-Com" businesses literally operated out of basements and garages of suburban homes and had no capital other than a promissory note of supposed future stock value. Then, at the stroke of midnight, 2000, the world held its breath—and nothing happened. January 1 came and went no differently than December 31. Demand vanished and the entire "Dot-Com" industry soon imploded. From March 10, 2000 through October 4, 2002, the NASDAQ Composite Index® plunged from its all-time high of 5048.62 to 1139.90, a loss of 77.42% in just 2½ years. Fifteen years later, it had still not fully recovered. More importantly, the bursting of the "Dot-Com" Bubble dragged everything else down with it. For example, over that same time, the S&P 500® lost 45.47% of its value.

It took five years for most of the major markets to recover. Then on October 12, 2007, the looming banking and home mortgage financial crisis reached the tipping point and markets crashed again. The S&P 500 alone lost 56.72% over sixteen months. By early January 2013, the S&P 500 had grown back to where it was on December 31, 1999. Thirteen years of investment performance with a net return of 0%.

So great was this volatility that it prompted Nobel Laureate William F. Sharpe and colleagues (Scott, Sharpe & Watson 2008) to re-examine Bengen's hypothesis. They concluded that adherence to the 4% Rule carried a 53% chance of failure—meaning a 53% chance an investor would outlive his/her money. Their findings have been subsequently echoed by many others (e.g., see Greene 2013, Pfau 2013, Weinreich 2013, Voegtlin and Pfau 2014).

Further, Finke, Pfau and Blanchette (2013) reported that in light of the historically low bond rates that resulted from the financial crisis of 2008 (the Great Recession), the sustainable expectations from the 4% Rule should be reduced to 2.8%. In other words, to sustain a long-term expectation of income, the amount of income one takes must be reduced by 30%. Translated that means a hypothetical investor with $300,000 who, under the 4% rule, would expect to generate income of $1000 per month, could now take only $700. Moreover, in light of low bond rates that dominated after the financial crisis of 2008, Finke (2013) raised the estimated the probability of failure to 57%.

In addition to problems associated with current market volatility, there are other fundamental errors with the 4% Rule:

1. **Increasing Human Life Expectancy.** Living longer raises the demand on return to sustain income. Voegtlin and Pfau (2014) note that in 1950, the average life expectancy of a 65 year-old male was 12.8 years and half would die before age 78. But, since the start of the new Millennium, the fastest growing demographic in the United States are people 65 and older (Administration on Aging, 2013) and by 2050 one in four men age 65 will live past age 85. Moreover, according to the U.S. Census Bureau (2011), over the next four decades, the population of people aged 90 and older is expected to more than quadruple. The longer a person lives, the more stress that places on a non-guaranteed income model to sustain itself.

2. **Historically low bond rates.** Normally, bond rates improve when stock markets are weak but that didn't happen with the financial crisis of 2008. Yields on 10-year Treasury Notes (bonds) fell from a high of 5.19% on July 6, 2007 to 2.17% by December 31, 2014. With low interest rates, the risk on bonds (not held to maturity) increases. Increasing risk on the portfolio reduces reliance on preserving principal after withdrawing regular income.

3. **Sequence of Returns Risk.** For those people who are "lucky" and start their retirement (based on 4% withdrawal) at the beginning of the "bull markets," the probability of success is far greater than those who start their retirement when the markets are at (or past) their peaks. Greene (2013), Voegtlin and Pfau (2014), citing analysis from T. Rowe Price, point out that an "unlucky" retiree who started income by the 4% Rule on January 1, 2000 would, by 2010, have lost a third of their total portfolio. Cot-

ton (2011) renamed "Sequence of Returns Risk" as "Probability of Ruin" and analyzed a number of mathematical scenarios to determine the chance of this and offered some various paths to reduce that risk.

But, consider the following. A retiree, "unlucky" enough to have retired in 2000, relying on the 4% Rule, would by 2015 have a little less than 10.6% of his initial sum left in the account. Even without another major market correction, he WILL run out of money within another 2 to 3 years. Worse, is that the total amount of money received over those 16 to 18 years would less than the initial starting sum. In other words, he'd have done better by transferring the entire retirement account into an interest-free checking account and merely spending the 4% Rule income until gone.

Unfortunately, as with any statistically-based model, academic paradigms of risk reduction and so forth, are no benefit the people who actually happen to be the ones who fall through the cracks. "Luck" has no place in retirement planning. Planning is about what's in one's ability to control, not "improve the odds, then hope."

4. **Inflation Risk.** According to the U.S. Bureau of Labor Statistics (2015), from 1995 through 2014 the average rate of inflation was 2.2% per year. Many people believe real inflation was actually much higher, but even taking the BLS statistic at face value, the long-term effects of inflation on income need are significant. The problem is that as the income dollar amount increases, the required return to replace that withdrawal increases at a greater rate. The relationship is actually logarithmic.

For example, a 4% withdrawal actually requires a 4.17% increase to break even. But after just ten years of inflation at 2.2%, a withdrawal of 4.97% is needed to receive the necessary income. And for that account to preserve principal, a return of 5.23% is required. After 20 years with just 2.2% inflation, income withdrawal requires 6.18% and 6.59% for recovery of principal. All these values assume constant growth with no market losses— ever. But, throw in a single 25% market correction, even in the first year the withdrawal rate would have jumped to 5.33%. But, that income withdrawal compounds on the capital loss, thereby reducing the total account value by 29.33%. To preserve principal, a one-year return of 40.85% is now required. And, without that recovery, every subsequent income payment further invades principal, accelerating shrinkage of the account until the account is depleted to $0. This is called *"Outliving your money."*

5. **It's not enough money.** Perhaps more than all the above, this is the biggest reason why the 4% Rule is a flawed retirement income strategy. Case-in-point, in 2015, according to multiple sources (e.g., U.S. Census Bureau, Census ACS, Sentier Research) the median income in the United States is around $56,000 per year. For a person working their entire lives at that rate, their Social Security benefit at Full Retirement Age would be approximately $1459/month or $17,508 per year. In order for that person to continue their lifestyle, they would need to generate an additional $38,492 in annual income. Without a sizeable pension, their 401(k) would need, at the time of retirement to be worth $962,300, three or more times greater than what estimates of the average 401(k) at retirement is actually worth. Even with a couple having equal joint income, the average retiree would come up short at 4% of investment. For example, assume a couple each generating $17,500 annual retirement income ($35,000) collectively and needing to generate a total household income of $56,000 per year, would need a retirement account of $525,000 to make up the $21,000 shortfall and that assumes NO increases for inflation. Add the supposed annual 3% inflation adjustment into the mix and the account needs to be closer to $800,000.

The sad conclusion to be drawn from this is that reliance on the 4% Rule is not advisable to anyone seeking a lifetime of income in retirement. It's why a growing number of leading economists and financial professionals admonish **DO NOT base retirement income on investment portfolios** because *"At the point of retirement, one bad year can ruin the rest of your life."*

MANDATORY LIQUIDATION

Within the United States, the largest single block of moneys is qualified retirement funds (IRA, 401(k), etc.). According to the Employee Benefit Research Institute (2015), by year-end of 2012, qualified retirement money totaled approximately $23.7 Trillion. Of that, more than $4.0 Trillion (17%) was in Defined Contribution Plans (including 401(k) Plans) and nearly $5.7 Trillion (24%) in traditional IRAs.

Current tax code mandates that a retiree who reaches the age of 70 ½ must begin a schedule of Required Minimum Distributions (RMDs) from a Qualified Retirement Plan (such as IRA and 401(k) plans). The amount of that mandatory liquidation is based on a table and the required percentage increases every year.

The distribution table starts at approximately 3.65% (by a divisor of 27.4) for a 70 year-old. The percentage that must be taken each year rises steadily upward from there through age 115. From there, it levels off at 52.63% per year (in case anyone was wondering). According to IRS life tables, the average life expectancy of a 70 year-old (unisex) is 17 years. For a person living to age 86, the average RMD is 4.88% per year. But, for someone who lives to age 90, that average RMD jumps to 5.28%. Note that all of these required distribution demands are well in excess of the 4% Rule, not to mention the newly revised estimate of 2.8%. However, because required minimum withdrawals are a percentage, not a dollar amount, as the IRA account value falls, the size of the RMD also decreases. As such, RMDs mathematically, CANNOT deplete an account to $0. However, the impact is to greatly reduce the total IRA account value and in "real life" a retiree could see a significant portion of his/her retirement money vanish into the "black hole" of math. Case-in-point:

Assume an investor, with an IRA worth $100,000 invested in the market (S&P 500 Index® without fees) on January 1, 2000, the same day as his 70th birthday. Also assume he lives 15 years to December 31, 2014. His IRA will be worth just $65,962.19. Even adding back in $49,370.68, the sum of all his RMDs, the total return is $115,332.87 or 0.96%. In comparison, the actual market without RMDs would have returned $137,999.80. Add in even investment modest fees, and the net return in the IRA would have been in negative territory.

It's important to note here that for IRA owners who DO NOT NEED income from their IRAs are in far less danger of depleting the entire account. However, it's unlikely that many, if not most investors would be "OK" with returns as dismal as just illustrated.

INCOME NOT ACCUMULATION

Merton (2014) does not mince words when it comes to planning. He states that a person approaching retirement must *"...refine the goals. A good framework in which to do this is to divide income needs into three categories:"* which he lists as:

1. *"Minimum Guaranteed Income"*

2. *"Conservatively Flexible Income"*

3. *"Desired Additional Income"*

The danger of outliving one's money falls squarely within the first category. In this instance, Merton's recommendations are specific and without waver. He states that Minimum Guaranteed Income *"must be inflation-protected and guaranteed for life..."* In other words, *"an infla-tion-protected life annuity from a highly rated insurance company..."*

For his categories two and three, Merton allows the moneys to be conservatively invested. However, these recommendations do not seem to account for the compounded problems associated of the 4% Rule in light of Required Minimum Distributions. Even though one will techni-cally not outlive his/her money by RMDs, the problems just described could mean much less money left over for beneficiaries. In conclusion, once Required Minimum Distributions begin, financial accounts that are exposed to the downsides of the stock market will not survive past the first significant correction (see Milevsky and Robinson 2005).

Clearly, some people don't care about beneficiaries. They'll justify that *"As long as I have money in life, after I'm dead, I don't care."* While there's obvious truth in this, it's also true that few of them gladly accept minimal or negative net return. In the end, everyone loves growth. It's what prompted Gordon Gekko (Michael Douglas' character in the 1987 film "Wall Street") to declare *"Greed is good."*

A BETTER (SMARTER) OPTION

Marcks and Kalamarides 2011 also reported that 72% of retirees believe they need to think differently about saving and planning for retirement. This, of course begs the question "What could be different?"

Marcks and Kalamarides, and Merton (2014) criticized corporate America for switching from Defined Benefit to Defined Contribution plans because they, and others, feel that retirement income planning should be based on a Defined Benefit Plan. This, of course begs the question, what *really* is a Defined Benefit Plan? The simple answer is it's a plan for a guaranteed lifetime of income to a worker and/or that worker's spouse; in other words an annuity. Merton in particular, specifically advises all retirees to rely on annuities as the foundation of retirement planning; what he calls the Minimum Guaranteed Income.

Returning to Merton's strong recommendation to rely on annuities as the cornerstone of his first category "Minimum Guaranteed Income," there is yet the open question: Could annuities also be suitable for the other two income categories? From the perspective of finance, Merton is a traditionalist. Conventional wisdom says "invest in the market for long-term growth." But this begs the larger question: *"Why take risk if it's not necessary?"* If it were possible to get comparable returns without the risk, why not do it?

So what then, is an annuity? There are as many opinions about annuities as there are different annuity products and it's difficult to make individual sense from the myriad of possibilities and opinions. According to the National Association of Insurance Commissioners (NAIC), the official definition of an annuity is an account from an insurance company designed to grow money for a period of time which can be converted into guaranteed lifetime income. In other words, an annuity is a "Personal Pension."

Within the world of annuities, there are two basic types: Variable and Fixed. Both work as future income generators but the similarities end there. In the broadest sense, a Variable Annuity is an investment portfolio with an insurance wrapper around it. They have many of the same risks as a traditional investment portfolio but generally with higher fees and impose other limitations. However, there are benefits as well. By contrast, a Fixed Annuity is a pure insurance product, the word "Fixed" referring not to "fixed" rate of return but to the safety and security of the account in that the annuity owner is never exposed to risk of loss due to market fluctuations.

The Fixed Index Annuity (FIA) was invented in 1995 to serve as a bridge between traditional fixed interest accounts that were safe and risk-based accounts that had much higher growth potential. By offering growth through indirect links to market indexes, they generate growth when markets rise but do not credit losses when markets fall. The obvious trade-off is that they cannot offer 100% of the gains on rising markets. If markets only went up and never fell, FIAs would be always take a back seat to markets for raw accumulation. But, during the crashes of 2000 and 2007, FIAs did not fall and when markets began to recover, they credited growth without having to wait for the markets to return to their former levels. The net result was long-term growth equal, if not better than what raw markets actually generated.

None-the-less, investors sometimes use the blunted upside potential as fodder to dismiss FIAs as a poor alternative to mutual funds. However, the facts speak otherwise. Morningstar's Director of Funds Research, Russel Kinnel (2014) reported that from 2003-2013, where the average Mutual Fund returned 7.3%, the average Mutual Fund investor gained just 4.8%, fully 2.5% less than theoretical. In large part this was attributed to imperfect timing by investors who sought to "beat the market."

To be fair, not all FIAs are created equal and some provide substantially better returns than others. But, the average FIA over that same time frame did not return significantly less than reported by Kinnel and some did better.

The value of *not* exposing an IRA in RMDs to market risk is far greater than might be supposed. For example, a hypothetical non-risk account (such as a FIA) averaging 5% per year in the face of RMDs after that same 15 years, would be worth $102,338.14 and have paid out $83,235.00. By comparison, this out-performed the risk IRA by nearly 61%.

None of this is meant to suggest that "all markets are bad" and "all annuities are good" any more than the other way around. However, it is a strong endorsement that Fixed Index Annuities should be a primary consideration for IRA moneys, especially if income from those retirement accounts is considered important.

SUMMARY

Retirement is a different phase of life than what exists during a person's working and earning years. It's a time when income comes not from what one does today and tomorrow, but what one did yesterday. As such, it is a finite and limited resource, which once gone, cannot be replaced. In short, one can regard the days of growing a retirement account as "Accumulation" and living off it as "Decumulation." Because this is a significant shift in function, there must also be an equal shift in application. In other words, a shift in thinking away from accepting the uncertainty of accumulation to embracing the certainty of income that cannot be outlived. Simply put, the 4% Rule is a truly a case of forcing a square peg into a round hole and convoluted rationalization by members of the investment industry to justify a continuance of "Accumulation" strategies in "Decumulation" planning is fundamentally flawed.

REFERENCES

Administration on Aging 2013. Administration for Community Living. U.S. Department of Health and Human Services. Dec. 31.

Bengen, William P. 1994. *Determining Withdrawal Rates Using Historical Data.* Journal of Financial Planning. October, pp. 171-180.

Bengen, William P. 2006. *Conserving Client Portfolios During Retirement.* FPA Press, Denver, CO.

Cooley, Philip L., Carl M. Hubbard, and Daniel T. Walz. 1998. *Retirement Savings: Choosing a Withdrawal Rate That Is Sustainable.* AAII Journal 10 (3):16–21.

Cotton, Dirk. 2015. *Sequence –of-returns Risk: A New Way of Looking at Spending or Saving Scenarios with Path Dependence.* Retirement Management Journal 5(1): 7-21

Employee Benefit Research Institute 2015. FAQs About Benefits—Retirement Issues. ebri.org online reports.

Finke, Michael. 2013. *Is the 4% Rule Folly?* AdvisorOne. April 29.

Finke. Michael S., Wade D. Pfau and David Blanchett. 2013. *The 4 Percent Rule is Not Safe in a Low-Yield World.* Journal of Financial Planning, Online Report.

Greene, Kelly. 2013. *Say Goodbye to the 4% Rule.* The Wall Street Journal online. Mar 3.

Marcks, Christine C. and John J. Kalamarides. 2011. *What Employers Lose in the Shift from Defined Benefit to Defined Contribution Plans... and How to Get it Back.* Retirement Management Journal 1(2): 9-21.

Merton, Robert C. 2014. *The Crisis in Retirement Planning.* Harvard Business Review, July-August: 3-10.

Milevsky, Moshe A. and Chris Robinson. 2005. *A Sustainable Spending Rate without Stimulation.* Financial Analysis Journal 61(6): 89-100.

Pfau, Wade D. 2013. *Breaking Free from the Safe Withdrawal Rate Paradigm: Extending the Efficient Frontier for Retirement Income.* AdvisorPerspectives.com. March 5.

Scott, Jason S., William F. Sharpe and John G. Watson. 2008. *The 4% Rule—At What Price.* Stanford.edu., April 3.

Shiller, Robert J. 2000. *Irrational Exuberance.* First Edition. Princeton University Press, Princeton, NJ

Shiller, Robert J. 2005. *Irrational Exuberance.* Second Edition. Princeton University Press, Princeton, NJ

United States Census Bureau 2011. Census Bureau Releases Comprehensive Analysis of Fast-Growing 90-and-Older Population. Nov 17.

United States Bureau of Labor Statistics 2015. Inflation Calculator.

Voegtlin, Rex and Wade D. Pfau. 2014. *Mitigating the Four Major Risks of Sustainable*

Inflation-Adjusted Retirement Income. A White Paper by the Annexus Research Institute.

Weinreich, Gill. 2013. *Finke Study Warns: 4% Retirement Rule Is Dead, Long Live Annuities.* AdvisorOne. January 17.

Section Three:
Understanding Qualified Plans

Utilizing Your Qualified Plan to Create Income Certainty

Kyle Winkfield

When you consider all of the ways that people prepare for retirement, the one that people focus on most often is an employer-sponsored Qualified Plan. A Qualified Plan is a financial instrument into which the federal government allows you to deposit pre-tax dollars. The money is allowed to grow tax-deferred, and taxes are paid upon withdrawal. Most people are familiar with the current incarnation of the Qualified Plan known as a defined contribution plan, of which the 401(k), 403(b) 457 and IRA are all examples.

Before the government introduced the framework for Qualified Retirement Plans, the employer-sponsored pension plan was the American hallmark of retirement security. There were enough companies that mismanaged their employee pension funds to such a degree that the government was encouraged to institute the 401 Qualified Retirement Plan IRS code in 1978. These new regulations provided for employees to both participate in and oversee the management of their retirement funds. As a result, more and more employers have been leaving the burden of retirement preparation and financing to their employees. Thus, the Baby Boomer generation is the first generation to have the freedom to plan and pay for their retirement. They are also, as it turns out, at considerable risk of not amassing adequate funds for their later years.

The purpose of a Qualified Plan is to provide an income supplement during retirement years for the account owner.[14] In recent decades, Americans have been saving less and less, in turn becoming more and more dependent on their qualified plans for their retirement financing. A popular misconception is that as long as part of each paycheck is going into a qualified plan, the plan owner will be adequately financed for their retirement. As a result, many of us are entering our retirement years with inadequate funding and a false sense of financial security. This toxic combination of unrealistic expectations, inadequate retirement funding and poor retirement planning must be avoided in order to insure that retirement is a pathway to fulfillment and not a train track heading over a cliff.

A compounding factor in this dilemma of underfunded retirees is that, along with increased control, we have also been granted more liquidity within our retirement accounts. This has led to a slow bleeding-off of funds over the years. We now find ourselves at the opening act of what may soon become the worst retirement crisis this country has ever seen. Robert C. Merton's July 2014 article published in the Harvard Business Review submitted a very strong case supporting just such a scenario.[15] John Bogle laid down a similar argument on the PBS show Frontline in February of 2013, in an episode entitled, "The Train Wreck Awaiting American[16] Retirement." The reality is that we're borrowing from our future to fund present needs and desires. The ability to access our retirement funds before we reach retirement age is turning out to be a grave threat to our investments' ability to grow.

Health threats and financial concerns run neck-and-neck in the race to the top of the list of retirement concerns for the Baby Boomer gener-

---

14 Martin Smith, The Retirement Gamble Facing Us All (Frontline, April, 2013), http://www.pbs.org

15 Robert C. Merton, "The Crisis In Retirement Planning," Harvard Business Review, (July-August 2014).

16 John Bogle, The Train Wreck Awaiting American Retirement, (Frontline, April 2013), http://www.pbs.org

ation (those born between 1946 and 1964).[17] According to AARP.com, retirementhomes.com and a recent survey by Allianz Life Insurance Company, we fear running out of money in our old age more than we fear dying.

A lack of prudence in our saving habits, a growing tendency to siphon-off our retirement funds for near-term spending and the regular cyclical nature of the financial markets appears to be a recipe for disaster. Our fortunes are shrinking. We built the strongest national economy that mankind has ever experienced, but poor education regarding our future needs combined with a lack of understanding about the immense value of well-informed retirement planning is driving an entire generation toward the old folks' poor house.

The most potent strategy one can develop in the face of this impending crisis involves the proper management of our two most valuable assets: our time and our money. Finding a financial advisor who understands how to leverage time in order to maximize asset growth so that savings will have the best chance to properly fund retirement, without drastically impacting current lifestyle is, the appropriate approach.

There are so many factors that must be considered on their own merit, as well as in conjunction with each other, that it only makes sense to utilize the knowledge and skills of a person, or better yet a team, dedicated to understanding retirement preparation and execution. As just plain smart and productive as this strategy might appear, it is not happening, at least on a scale large enough to avoid the coming troubles for the Boomer generation. You, however, can drastically improve your prospects for a fully funded retirement, regardless of the plight of those around you.

Let's take a deeper look at qualified plans, both pros and cons, from a retirement income planning perspective.

---

17 Allianz Life Insurance Company, Retirement in America Will Never Be the Same (Reclaiming the Future Study, 2010), http://www.allianzlife.com

Qualified Plan Facts:

- Contributions are made pre-tax (taxes are deferred until the time of withdrawals)

- Those under the age of 50 can contribute up to $18,000/year,

- Those over 50 can contribute up to $24,000/year, known as "catch-up contributions (per new 2015 limits),

- Money removed from the plan before the age of 59 ½ may face a 10% penalty

- There can be income restrictions on participation (Roth IRAs are only accessible if your household makes less than a certain annual income)

Qualified Plan Misunderstandings:

- Qualified plans are automatically safe places to save money. While they do offer certain advantages, the funds invested can still be exposed to significant market risks that can compromise principal investment, earnings and future growth,

- Most Americans think that their qualified plans recover from market losses or from withdrawals because more contributions are being deposited. Unfortunately, contributions are not the same as investment gains, but are often confused as such when investors look at their year-end statements without delving into the details.

When it comes to retirement planning, it is vital that we focus on a realistic impression of our qualified plan's capacity to build value while protecting our assets. The ultimate goal in retirement planning is to secure the retirement lifestyle of our choosing. Granted, we may have to adjust our lifestyle choices to accurately reflect our ability to pay for them, but such is the nature of planning. Lifestyle security, attainable through income certainty, involves the creation of a guaranteed income stream that you cannot outlive. In other words, you have dedicated a portion of your employment income to build investments that will provide a stream of income that will support your retirement lifestyle regardless of your lifespan.

If you are like a lot of us, you've been diligent in contributing to your qualified plan, have weathered some losses, and are now looking at a good-sized nest egg. Now what? The reality is that most people at this "now what?" stage focus on the wrong things. The most popular distractions are rate of return and net worth. While the issues of growth and net worth are vital, it is even more important to make safety the first priority. Asset protection is everything. You built it. You need it. Secure it. We will delve into specific tools and strategies shortly.

Your next consideration is determining the best ways to turn this well defended collection of assets into reliable retirement income. Your retirement accounts are somewhat of a financial report card for how you have done over the last 20, 30, 40 years. If you do not have a passing grade, guess what? You are not retiring! Sure, there may be a retirement party, but the next day you could be starting your new job at the mall because you don't have enough money to support yourself.

The real questions that you should be asking, in this order, are how do I preserve what I have saved and how can I create a guaranteed income stream from these savings?

Here are some additional vital questions to ask when considering your qualified plan and retirement income:

- How much income do I want/need from retirement savings?

- Do I need my qualified plan money in order to support my retirement lifestyle?

- Do I want a guaranteed paycheck coming from my retirement savings?

- Do I want my paycheck to be based on the popular 4% rule of regular fund dispersals?

- How will a downturn in the market impact my retirement paycheck?

- If I choose to stay in the market and bare the risk, what is my contingency recovery strategy?
- At what level do losses become unacceptable?
- If I lose my qualified plan savings due to market loss, how would my lifestyle be impacted?
- How do I feel about losing $25,000? $250,000?
- What taxes apply to early qualified plan withdrawals?
- Is there a tax bracket into which I want to fit in retirement?

The most important thing to do, particularly in the late stages of retirement preparation, is to avoid risk. While it's popular to react with a gambler's emotions and focus on high returns that hold the promise of big presents under the retirement tree, this approach can be ruinous. Remember, time and money are your most important assets, and time is running out. There are several places to grow your savings while also ensuring safety and liquidity. Some even offer a guaranteed stream of income even after your savings have run dry. Warren Buffet has famously warned that it is important to remember that first, do not lose money, and, second, do not lose money.

The following example can be used to illustrate the impact of market losses on your retirement:

Investor A has $10,000 and selects an account that is guaranteed to receive a 1% return each year. Investor B has $10,000 and selects an account that is market-based and is said to receive a 20% average return. Who will have more money at the end of 2 years?

	Principle	Year 1	Year 2	Ending Balance
Investor A	$10,000	$10,000 + 1% = $10,100	$10,100 + 1%	$10,201
Investor B	$10,000	$10,000 + 90% (market gain) = $19,000	$19,000 + (-50% market loss)	$9,500

Math: 90%—50% = 40% / 2 (years) = 20%.—According to the math, Investor B did average a 20% rate of return. Did the math equate to real money for Investor B? After two years, Investor B lost all of his gains and some of his principle. While Investor B might have the time to "recover" his losses, the market is not guaranteed and how many times can Investor B afford to take these kinds of losses with his retirement savings before he's out of time, and out of money?

Investor A chose a "conservative" account and while his gains are not awe-inspiring, slow and steady wins the race over time. Moral: math does not equate to real money. When it comes to income certainty, you're looking for yield or a guaranteed payout factor, not an average rate of return.

There are several places to grow your savings while also ensuring safety and liquidity, including ones that offer a guaranteed income stream, even after your savings have run dry. Evaluating all possible options is the most important first step, and you'll want to consult advisors who can offer a variety of safe ones.

When it comes to savings held in a qualified plan (which typically contain traditional market risk products), the possibility of outliving the income-producing capability of these savings is known as "Sequence of Returns Risk." Sequence of returns risk is only a factor in market-based investment products and is best described as the threat of stunted asset growth due to poor market performance early in the asset's life cycle. The primary threat to your sequence of returns is reduction of your principal. The two primary threats to your principal are market fluctuations and withdrawals

As you enter the distribution/spending phase of retirement (when you begin to draw an income from your retirement account), if your funds remain in an account subject to market risk, your dollars are still potentially earning and potentially disappearing; that's when Sequence of Returns Risk also enters the picture. How your withdrawals coincide with the market ups and downs in a year can result in one of two outcomes: your money lasting longer or running out sooner. What happens in a period of a few years can impact whether your money lasts until you're 81 or 91—that's a big deal.

Prominent Finance Professor Moshe A. Milevsky illustrated this phenomenon in the chart titled "What stop did you get on the retirement merry-go-round?" in his paper Retirement Ruin and the Sequencing of Returns.[18] The Return Sequence column indicates three years of market returns (applied to your retirement dollars) and how their order of occurrence within a three-year period directly impacts the age at which your account runs out of money.

What stop did you get on the retirement merry-go-round?

Return Sequence	Ruin Age	+/- Months
+7%, +7%, +7%...	86.50	
+7%, -13%, +27%...	83.33	-38
+7%, +27%, -13%...	89.50	+36
-13%, +7%, +27%...	81.08	-65
+27%, +7%, -13%...	94.92	+101

*Assumes $9,000 spending per year.

http://www.ifid.ca/pdf_newsletters/pfa_2006feb_sequencing.pdf

What does this mean for you? When preparing your retirement plan, look for accounts that seek to eliminate sequence of returns risk. They will have the following characteristics: preservation of capital (you cannot lose your principal nor risk your prior gains), and a guaranteed income stream specifically designed so that the recipient cannot outlive it.

---

18 Moshe A. Mievsky, Retirement Ruin and the Sequencing of Returns, (2006): 6. http://www.ifid.ca

Annuities

When making a decision regarding safety of principal and the protection of your earnings, consider what safeguards you currently have in place. In other words, how risky is your current retirement portfolio? If the market corrected and lost significant value, how would that impact your retirement savings and resulting lifestyle choices? Annuities have been utilized for centuries to provide guaranteed income and principal protection for the annuity owner and annuitant. These two distinctions, safety of capital and assurance of income, are what set an annuity apart from other market-based products that typically do not provide guarantees. An important question to always consider when managing your retirement income accounts is, "At any point, will it be acceptable to risk the loss of some or all of my savings?"

An Annuity may be right for you if:

- You would like to establish a guaranteed retirement income stream (guaranteed paycheck in retirement).

- You cannot afford to lose money or simply don't want to lose money.

- Your retirement nest egg is currently in "speculation" mode (subject to market losses).

- You would like to grow your money without risk to principal or risk to prior gains.

- You would like to create a guaranteed income stream as well as have the option to walk away at the end of an established time frame, having suffered no monetary loss.

Complementing your Qualified Plan investment portfolio with a safety-focused instrument like an annuity can help you adjust your prospects for securing income, regardless of market performance or other factors that might affect your retirement account. An annuity kills two birds with one stone. It knocks out Sequence of Returns Risk because it can give you a fixed rate of return and it provides guaranteed income for life. Even if you don't get an annuity with a fixed rate of return, you still have the assurance of the guaranteed income for your lifetime.

The retirement of the Baby Boomer Generation ushers us into the first wave of DIY (do it yourself) retirement planning. The defined benefit plans of yesteryear are few and far between, and their numbers are fading with each tick of the clock. These types of changes are placing responsibility for lifestyle maintenance through the retirement years on the individual retiree and lessening the burden for the employer. In order to realistically address our individual retirement needs and do what is best for ourselves, families and community, we have to seek out the best sources of accurate information and guidance in order to develop a workable plan populated with the products that address our needs for safety, value and dependable income.

What You Should Know Before Investing in a 401(k)

By Kyle O'Dell

The media has become bipolar. One day Americans are in a savings crisis, the next they're subject to the government taxing them more for saving too much. This indecisiveness and mixed messaging leads many Americans to massive confusion about their financial futures.

Sure, Americans are more educated on financial matters than past generations. But the entire world of personal finance, retirement and the like has become increasingly complex over time too. We know more, but there's a lot more to know! To make things harder, the "conventional wisdom" often changes, and as things become popular, we get more varied information.

For instance, one savings vehicle with mass appeal is the 401(k). According to the *American Benefits Council,* more than 80% of Americans have a retirement plan through their employer, with the 401(k) being the premier Defined Contribution Plan among full-timers.

Of course with anything popular, criticism and doubt are not far behind. However, if a person knows how to manage his or her expectations and what the outcome can be, the future result can be easier to digest. The 401(k) is no exception.

Building retirement savings with a 401(k) is popular because employee contributions are often matched by employers (up to a certain amount) and the process is relatively simple. Employees determine the pre-tax dollars they want to contribute, and never notice the money coming out of their check—out of sight, out of mind. The process continues and money accumulates throughout the years. On top of that, the funds in the plan are legally protected from creditors and debtors.

This seems like an easy, turnkey savings solution. Great concept, right? In theory, yes.

What I described above was the scenario Congress had in mind in 1974 with the Employee Retirement Income Security Act (ERISA). The intention was to make investing for retirement easier and more profitable for the average person.

There were safeguards put in place to help employees, like a penalty for dipping into the account before age 59 ½. The hope is/was that the individual would leave it alone over time. The act permits the owner to defer taxes on certain retirement plans, including 401(k) plans, until money is withdrawn in retirement, with the expectation that people will be in lower tax brackets when they retire.

But I don't want to discourage you. That scenario isn't a pipe dream of the past. It can happen for you today, if you know how to get the most from your 401(k).

Are you maximizing your 401(k) in the most efficient way?

Most Americans decide the day they are hired into a company how much they'll put in their 401(k) and they keep contributing. And why not? At the time of hire, the entire arrangement is generally explained in a manner where the company will match contributions and employees will max out at a certain amount every year.

However, an annual account review can really maximize the end result. Isn't that what everyone wants? Here's how you can start today.

I have a checklist when I'm meeting with a client for the first time. I hate to use the "School House Rock" cliché, but "Knowledge is Power." The more you know, the more you can maximize your future earnings. And as crazy as it sounds, you may actually enjoy the process along the way.

1. **On the anniversary of your hire date, pull out the 401(k) documents. Put this date on your calendar!**

    a. More often than not, this is when you'll negotiate a pay raise or bonus structure. Is there an opportunity to increase your 401(k) contribution too?

2. **Look at the current tax rate.**

    a. If it's decreasing, should you be paying taxes on this money right now, especially if you're already maxing out the 401(k) contribution? The IRS can change the rate at any time, for any reason.

    b. If the tax rate is lower, save just enough in the 401(k) to match what the company contributes. Then put your net income in a tax-advantaged vehicle like a Roth IRA, municipal bond or a properly structured life insurance policy.

3. **Take the time to figure out what retirement looks like in your current state.**

    a. No one can predict the future, but paying attention to the tax bracket you're currently in, the pace you're contributing/saving, and what your personal overhead looks like is important. Examine your current bills too and the duration of any loan commitments. These are important pieces of your personal retirement scenario!

        i.   For example, if you have a 30-year mortgage that's 10 years from being paid off, and you plan to retire in 12 years, you won't be able to count the mortgage interest as a tax deduction once you have paid it off. The reason 401(k)s are of benefit is because you're deferring taxes until a time you think you'll be in a lower tax bracket. It's so important to keep expenses manageable in retirement.

4. **Use the 401(k) Optimizer program**

    a. This program from Howard Capital in Roswell, GA, is $79 a month(As of August 2015) and is worth every penny. Simply put, it helps monitor what the market is doing by examining the economy as a whole. The program takes a defensive approach to your 401(k) regarding market downturns and updates you if it detects a possible threat. It helps employees learn to manage the portfolio inside their 401(k) accounts. Some financial advisors will give you free access to the program if you're already working with them, so be sure to ask.

This checklist is a starting point, especially if you've been with the same company for a while or plan to stay there for years to come. But recent years have produced lots of "job hopping" in the employment market.

To be sure, today's world is not like the one our parents came up in. People aren't content with mediocrity and stagnant wages in exchange for job security. And major companies aren't so concerned with how long an employee has been at one place. They want strong talent and proven results. If the employee can provide all of this, firms have no problem paying them what they're worth.

So what does this new, dynamic environment mean to the employee who wants to maximize his or her 401(k)?

The Job Hopper

The new generation doesn't settle for anything less than what they think they deserve. Back in 2013, CNN reported that people are "job hopping to keep from getting stagnant wages." The one example they cited was a gentleman who received a 31% pay increase within two years. To me, that's proof positive that employers will pay more for strong talent and proven results.

In terms of retirement savings, the question has to be asked—should employees start a 401(k) everywhere they go? Maybe.

If the employer is matching, it's great for the employee to maximize any revenue source that helps their personal bottom line. But it's wise to understand the differences between plans at different companies. If the

401(k) at a previous employer has lower fees and expenses than the new company, leave it there. This savings vehicle was designed to meet *your* needs, not your employer's needs.

Of course you may start a new 401(k) at the new company, especially if you're being paid more in the new position. However, if you aren't contributing the max to the 401(k), try to live the same as you were on your old, smaller salary, then save your new "extra" money. If you can stay in the smaller-budget mindset for a few years and continue saving, the compounding effect on the growth can dramatically improve your future financial forecast.

If the job-hopping method in life is building to an annual occurrence for you, it may be time to figure out how to take all the various retirement accounts and put them under one umbrella. People often think that's not an option, which is a common misconception. It couldn't be farther from the truth. Consolidating accounts helps simplify the savings process, making portfolio management more efficient. This will likely become a more popular strategy, as job-hopping seems to be here to stay.

What Are the Challenges with Investing in a 401(k)?

I'm about to make an oxymoron, but people who have saved too much in a 401(k) can be penalized with taxes.

What?

You probably read that thinking, "I worked so hard to save and contribute, how can that happen?" Looking at recent tax code changes, it seems the government needs a way to fund past obligations. Think about that. Wars haven't been paid for, and social programs cost more and more over time. More than 10,000 Baby Boomers are moving into retirement every day. We've been told they haven't saved enough because, as a nation, we still to pay for Medicaid, Medicare and Social Security.

Where do you think the money for all that will come from? Taxes!

It's logical to think the people who didn't save enough won't change tax brackets, they will still live in the 10% to 15% arena. Unfortunately, it's the people who did everything right (by saving) who are being penalized, as we'll see below.

Eventually Uncle Sam is going to want the taxes he let you defer for so long in retirement accounts, which is a challenge for savers. Americans know that at age 70 ½ they must start taking their required minimum distributions (RMDs) from 401(k) or IRA accounts. The percentage begins at 3.65% and increases annually.

If people saved too much in these accounts, they're forced to take out more than they want/need in RMDs, which in turn forces them in to a higher tax bracket, resulting in a higher tax bill! Some may believe this isn't a bad problem to have, but when you're on a fixed income, any large, unexpected expense can send the budget into a tailspin.

There is a solution, however, and it's simpler than you think. The answer really is that people need to be strategic and plan their financial future.

For instance, currently couples at age 65 are entitled to a $22,700 standard deduction on their tax returns. If a married couple has $622,000 in an IRA, the minimum distribution would be $22,700, based on a 3.65% RMD rate. The deduction would cancel out the income, therefore not putting the couple into a higher tax bracket. That's what I mean by strategic planning!

As mentioned earlier, that percentage will increase every year. But good planning takes that into account. It's incredibly important to pay attention in the accumulation phase of your retirement savings journey to see how much a tax-deferred investment vehicle grows. As it nears certain thresholds, changes are needed to maximize efficiency and aim to keep your money away from Uncle Sam.

Success in Your Golden Years

From that first job until the twilight of our careers, retirement needs to be a priority throughout life. Consult the right experts on your journey, including a qualified financial advisor and tax attorney, and you'll be well positioned for retirement success.

When working with your advisors, never forget that clarity is king. Be clear about what you want in life—and what you don't want—and work toward those goals with a strategic plan, making adjustments as needed. More specifically, understand what you're investing in (demand it!) and be as efficient as possible cost-wise.

It's really about determining what you want in retirement and making it attainable based on your current situation. Remember, building towards your dreams is a journey, and success doesn't happen overnight.

Section Four:
Tax Efficient Retirement Income

Managing Your Tax Brackets

By: Kyle O'Dell

Supposedly there are two certainties in life—one of them being taxes. The problem is tax rates are uncertain in amount and duration, meaning we don't know for sure what rate we'll be charged, or for how long. The reality is that tax rates have actually been as high as 94%. Between 1936 and 1981, the top federal income tax bracket never dropped below 70%!

Did you know that if you had prepared properly during your working years, you could have put yourself in position to enjoy a 0% tax bracket during retirement?

In order to make that happen, you must understand the three types of accounts where you can save your money—Taxable, Tax-Deferred and Tax-Free.

I like to think of each as a bucket that you fill with money. It's simple, but it's also effective. Let's talk about the three buckets where you should save your money and how much you should have in each one.

Bucket 1—Taxable Money

You may be asking yourself, why would I put money somewhere that is going to be taxed? Good question. In this instance, you're trading taxability for control. Taxable money means liquidity, use and control of your cash at all times. Anytime you have tax benefits you are going to give up some liquidity.

This bucket isn't the place to accumulate cash for retirement; it's your emergency fund! So you need it to be accessible. But realize that too much money in this bucket will cause an unnecessarily high tax burden. However, having too little could cause a problem if you need cash. You have to find the right balance. One of the most common problems I see affluent clients encounter is having too much taxable money. It seems like a nice problem to have, but what is the true cost of having too much in this bucket?

Let's say you have $200,000 of non-qualified cash invested in mutual funds and the account grows by 10%, giving you an account balance of $220,000 at the end of the year. In most years you will receive a 1099 tax bill on that account because of the turnover rate within the mutual fund. Because the mutual fund is buying and selling shares of stock (aka turnover), the tax gets passed onto you. Let's say the tax bill you receive is $4,000. That's not so bad, considering your account has $220,000 in it.

But consider this...

On April 15, when the tax bill is due, how do you pay it? Do you make a withdrawal from your mutual fund of $4,000? Or do you write the check and pay the bill with the cash in your checking account?

Contrary to what you may think, you should pay the $4,000 bill with the cash sitting in your checking account. If you make the mutual fund withdrawal, here's what you haven't taken into account- it wasn't just the $4,000 you lost to Uncle Sam UNNECESSARILY, but also the ability to earn interest on that $4,000!

Say you're 45 years old and could have kept the $4,000 and invested it over your lifetime. Assuming you live until age 85, at a 6% rate of return, your $4,000 could have grown to $41,143!

Uncle Sam loves your taxable account! If your $220,000 account continues to grow and you keep paying this tax every year, how much money are you giving away to Uncle Sam unnecessarily over your lifetime? For many families, it can add up to tens or even hundreds of thousands of dollars.

Also, by having too much money in this bucket, your Social Security could be taxed. That's another reason the right balance in the Taxable Money bucket is so important.

So how much should you have in this bucket? Well, it should be your emergency fund. As a rule of thumb, most families should have 6 months of income in this account. But the truth is, you need enough in there to help you sleep well at night.

Bucket 2—Tax-Deferred Money

Accounts in this bucket come in many different forms. It could be your 401(k), 403(b), 457, TSP, Simple IRA, Traditional IRA, Keogh, etc.

What all of these accounts have in common is that they postpone the tax hit until you withdraw the money. Then you'll pay taxes based on your current Marginal Tax Bracket. That's why Tax-Deferred accounts are the most popular place for most Americans to build retirement savings.

But the one thing most people don't really think enough about regarding these types of accounts is that they have been postponing the tax on all their retirement dollars for many years. And when they go to withdraw that money, the tax bill could be quite large. Let's take a look at an example of why Uncle Sam doesn't just like Tax-Deferred accounts— he loves them!

Say you were going to go into business with your cousin and you were going to put up all the money to start the business, but it resulted in just a 75% ownership stake. Your cousin gets a 25% ownership stake, even though he didn't really do anything to help you fund your company. On opening day, your cousin said he loves his 25% ownership stake, but when *you* retire and sell the company, he may need more than a 25% stake to help pay *his* bills in retirement.

Now if that were the deal, would you go into business with your cousin? No, you wouldn't!

But this is exactly the arrangement you have with Uncle Sam. If his bills continue to increase (Social Security, Medicare, Medicaid, interest on our national debt, etc.), he will let you know if he wants more from this bucket in the future.

When you retire, is there a way to get the money out of your Tax-Deferred account and not pay any taxes? The answer is yes, if you've planned properly. Here's a simplified example.

Prior to retiring, most married couples enjoy tax deductions that come from retirement plan contributions (i.e., 401(k)), children, mortgage interest and charities. But what happens to all these deduction when you retire? The children are grown, your house may be paid off, you're no longer contributing to your qualified plan at work and you don't receive a deduction for the children, even if they're still living at home.

Before retirement, most families itemize their deductions (kids, mortgage interest, etc.). But during retirement, those deductions are gone, so most families take the Standard Deduction. If the Standard Deduction is $14,800, plus $3,950 for yourself and $3,950 for your spouse, then the total would be $22,700. Typically the Standard Deduction increases by about 2.5% each year.

These numbers are important for you to know because they help answer our original question of how much should be in your Tax-Deferred account.

Well the answer is fairly simple to figure, but not easily accomplished. The amount you want to withdraw from your Tax-Deferred account should be equal to the Standard Deduction. In our example, the Standard Deduction is $22,700, so you should withdraw $22,700 from your Tax-Deferred accounts. The Standard Deduction will negate the withdrawal in terms of tax liability.

Before I give you the formula for figuring out how much money you and your spouse should have combined in all your Tax-Deferred accounts, there is one more important piece to this puzzle that we need to discuss. At age 70 ½, you'll have Required Minimum Distributions (RMD's) on all your qualified accounts. This is the amount that Uncle Sam is requiring you to withdraw from your Tax-Deferred accounts.

Why would the government require you to withdraw money? Because you haven't been taxed on this money and the government wants its share! So when you get to 70 ½, you want your RMD to be equal to the Standard Deduction, therefore offsetting that withdraw as it relates to tax liability.

Many people contribute to their Tax-Deferred accounts because of the tax deduction, and this is usually on the advice of their CPA. Many CPAs are simply trying to get your taxes to be as low as possible each year. They typically don't look years ahead, when the consequences of decades of deferred taxes could have a dramatic effect on your retirement.

Without further ado, here's the formula:

The first year that you have RMDs at 70 ½, you'll be required to withdraw 3.65% from your qualified accounts. That means that for every $100,000 you've saved, you'll have to withdraw $3,650. The $3,650 will then get added to your tax return as income. If the Standard Deduction is $22,700, take 22,700 and divide it by .0365, which will give you the maximum dollar amount you should have in your Tax Deferred accounts. In our example, the answer is $621,917.

$$\frac{22{,}700}{.0365} = 621{,}917$$

The Standard Deduction typically increases by about 2.5% per year. If you are still several years from 70 ½, then the Standard Deduction may be higher by the time you reach that age. But be prepared for it not only as you approach RMDs, but the whole time you're taking them!

Bucket 3—Tax-Free

This is by far the most underutilized area to accumulate savings for most families. There are several Tax-Free bucket account options, but the question is, how much money should you have here in order to achieve a 0% tax bracket? The answer is all your remaining money. Here's how.

Most families are only aware of Roth IRAs as a way to fill the Tax-Free bucket. Roth IRAs provide tax-free funds, as long as you follow the

IRS guidelines of not withdrawing until age 59 ½ and establishing your Roth IRA five years prior to distributions.

But did you know there are other tax-free places to accumulate cash, like municipal bonds issued by your state of residence and properly-designed life insurance policies? All three can fill this bucket.

Roth IRAs

I like Roth accounts as places to accumulate tax-free growth, but they're not perfect solutions. For example, the amount you can contribute is limited. Also, if you earn too much, you can't contribute to a Roth IRA at all. Lastly, you can't access the money without penalty until age 59 ½.

Another option is to convert your current Traditional IRA to a Roth IRA. In order to convert, you'll have to pay a tax at the time of conversion. This means that if you have $200,000 in a Traditional IRA and you want to convert $50,000 of it to a Roth, you will pay taxes on the converted $50,000 portion. But you'll never pay taxes again on the converted money as long as you follow the Roth IRA rules.

The problem with converting is often the source of the tax funds. You want to pay the conversion tax with non-qualified cash, but not everyone has enough cash sitting around to pay the tax bill. And remember, you don't want to have too much money in non-qualified accounts or risk being bumped into a higher tax bracket later. The amount you convert is considered income, which could increase your taxes.

In general, I like Roth IRAs for their tax-free growth ability. They usually make sense for families who qualify to contribute to them. But I'm not a fan of Roth IRAs necessarily when it comes to converting into them from a Traditional IRA—conversions have to make sense and be executed properly. Bottom line—every client situation is different, so make a decision on what makes most sense for you!

Municipal Bonds

Like Roth IRAs, municipal bonds can also be Tax-Free bucket holdings, as long as you purchase the correct type of bonds. That said, I'm not a huge fan of municipal bonds solely as a tax-free investment for two reasons.

One is the risk associated with purchasing bonds from the municipality in which you live. There are recent instances of cities entering bankruptcy! The other reason is the potential for rising interest rates and inflation. Rates have to go up sometime, right? For the typical investor, there are just too many risks and hoops to jump through when looking at municipal bonds.

Life Insurance

The third way to fill the Tax-Free bucket is to accumulate savings inside of a properly structured life insurance policy. Now I know what most of you are thinking, "life insurance?!" Using a life insurance policy isn't for everyone, but it can be a great place to accumulate cash that will help you manage your tax bracket in the future. Now we all know the primary purpose of life insurance is life insurance (the death benefit), but did you know that while you are alive, life insurance also has living benefits?

To properly design a life policy for the living benefits, while knowing we have the death benefit protection, make efficiency a priority. And by that I mean keep the cost of insurance as low as possible. If a family has accumulated the correct amount of cash in each of the first two buckets—Taxable and Tax-Deferred—the balance of the money should go into the Tax-Free bucket, and properly-designed permanent life insurance policies are great investment options.

Let's look at a visual example of how most people buy any type of insurance, whether it's auto, health or life insurance. Put simply, we purchase the coverage amount that we need and then we shop around for the lowest premium.

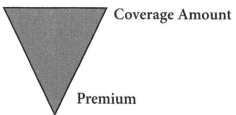

Coverage Amount

Premium

But with our goal of using the policy mostly for its living benefits, we want to flip the typical insurance buying habit.

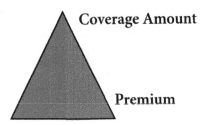

Coverage Amount

Premium

Consider a $200,000 policy, as the owner pays the premium every year and they get another year closer to life expectancy the insurance companies risk is decreased. Therefore the cost of insurance is decreased as the cash value goes up. This is a very simple explanation, but the idea is that a properly designed policy can be a very efficient place to accumulate cash.

We won't go into detail as to how interest crediting works inside the policy, but understand that there are policies that have traditionally paid out 3-7% in interest, depending on the type of policy and type of crediting method that was chosen. That's a 3-7% guaranteed return on your money, as long as you abide by the terms of the policy.

Bottom Line—Don't dismiss life insurance as an option for this third bucket and consider discussing it with an advisor.

Plan to Properly Fill the Buckets, Manage Taxes

Mike Tyson famously said, "Everyone thinks they have a plan until they get punched in the mouth."

That's a succinctly powerful point, and it's certainly true with our finances. Everyone thinks their finances are in good order until the market drops or taxes rise. But the truth is, the future is uncertain. Of course, we can't tell exactly what will happen. But we can plan for the unknown as much as possible to position ourselves for retirement success, including minimizing our tax liabilities.

Expanding social programs and soaring debt seem to point to higher future taxes—the equivalent of a fiscal uppercut. When that happens, how will you react? Put another way, have you created a plan to minimize the risk of a future tax increase?

With the three buckets filled properly, you can manage your tax bracket in retirement and actually experience the "being in a lower tax bracket" most people assume will happen, but often doesn't. By working with a professional to structure and fill your financial buckets, almost anyone can achieve a 0% tax bracket in retirement, or come very close.

Required Minimum Distributions (RMD) and Your 70.5 Birthday

By James B. Merklinghaus

My wife's family friend Mabel is quite a few years older than us, and she was among my early clients when I started my first firm. When we threw her a surprise 70.5 birthday party instead of a more traditional 70, she got the joke.

She didn't even mind the "Happy RMD" on her cake or the "Don't forget your RMD" balloons. Being a friend and client, Mabel was one of the most knowledgeable laypersons about retirement planning and the ever-changing rules. She beamed at the theme because everything was going according to plan. It was indeed a Happy RMD for Mabel!

What is a Required Minimum Distribution (RMD)

Mabel is at our house a lot, stuck talking to me about one of my favorite subjects—retirement—before my wife can whisk her away. She had no choice but to memorize that at age 70.5, there was a Required Minimum Distribution (RMD) that she had to withdraw from her IRA accounts.[19]

The RMD could've been a disaster if she had forgotten it had existed. But since we planned ahead, her money is tucked away for a later time when perhaps she might need it. It is growing safe, tax-deferred, and

---

19 http://www.irs.gov/Retirement-Plans/Plan-Participant,-Employee/Retirement-Topics-Required-Minimum-Distributions-(RMDs)

even available for her daughter Kate, since that's what's she's chosen. Kate has it further secured in a tax-deferred option that can grow for decades. This is a family that plans ahead.

Now, I'm not suggesting we all throw RMD parties for our friends. Mable's family and pals got the joke and didn't mind the change of theme from "over the hill," because, let's face it, 70.5 is hardly old these days. Everyone at that party had decided that IRS rules being the rules, it's much better to be forced to withdraw money than have no money to withdraw, or, to have been withdrawing all along just to get by.

What are the rules?

Most tax-advantaged retirement accounts, including IRAs, 401(k)s and business-sponsored retirement plans, have RMD rules. But the rules vary from one account to another. Once you start taking RMDs you must keep taking them every year by December 31.[20]

RMDs are calculated by dividing an account's balance by an IRS-calculated life expectancy figure. So, the lower your account balance, the lower your RMD. And since excess distributions lower your account balance, they also indirectly lower next year's RMD.[21]

According to a new report from the Employee Benefit Research Institute (EBRI), people realize that by delaying and minimizing withdrawals, they maximize the amount of money they can continue to grow on a tax-deferred basis for as long as possible.[22] The report indicates that a great many people delay IRA withdrawals from until forced because of RMDs.

Interestingly, mostly retired folks don't delay RMDs because they don't need or want their money, the report says. They are simply avoiding tax liability, and doing whatever it takes to hang on to their money,

20 http://www.irs.gov/Retirement-Plans/Plan-Participant,-Employee/Retirement-Topics-Required-Minimum-Distributions-(RMDs)
21 http://www.ebri.org/pdf/PR1132.IRAs.15July15.pdf
22 http://www.irs.gov/Retirement-Plans/Retirement-Plans-FAQs-regarding-Required-Minimum-Distributions#8

figuring they'll need it even more when they're older. Their bottom line goal is to avoid outliving their assets.

Uncle Sam

Mabel, like many of our family and friends entering their senior years, express more gratitude for their health and loved ones than anything else. But money always comes up. Paying taxes isn't the worst thing that can happen to a person, they say. But why pay more taxes when you can pay more to yourself—and your loved ones?

Not needing your RMD is a wonderful position to be in, but it can also be a double-edged sword, even a triple-edged sword. If you, like Mable, are in the enviable position of not needing your retirement savings by the time you are 70.5, that is reason enough to kick up your heels.

The only downside is you are forced to withdraw a minimum amount and could be in a position of paying more taxes than you anticipated.[23] Don't forget—you've been holding on to that money, watching it grow tax-deferred. Our government wants its share.

If you forget to take that minimum withdrawal, the penalty is 50 percent of what you should have taken out, plus any tax you would have owed.[24] That's a steep penalty for forgetting. There are exceptions—but they are numerous and require much proof.[25]

That's why planning is important. If Mable had left her money in IRAs, it's likely the RMD would've been a tax—and penalty—surprise.

Avoiding the RMD—or—'I forgot' penalty and tax

Mable, not needing an income stream from her retirement accounts, was in a perfect position for a Qualified Longevity Annuity Contract (QLAC).

---

23 http://www.irs.gov/Retirement-Plans/Retirement-Plans-FAQs-regarding-Required-Minimum-Distributions#8

24 http://www.irs.gov/irb/2014-30_IRB/ar07.html

25 http://www.treasury.gov/press-center/press-releases/Pages/jl2448.aspx

QLACs came on the scene in August 2014 precisely for people who want to keep investments in place, tax deferred, up until age 85. The vehicle was created because the IRS feared people were living longer than their money would last.[8]

With a QLAC, participants can defer $125,000 or 25 percent of the account balance (whichever is less). Account balances for QLAC purchases are either transfers or rollovers from other existing qualified accounts, such as an IRA, 401(k), 403(b) and the like. The insurance application includes forms that facilitate and finalize the transfers or rollovers. Penalties occur only if these transactions are mishandled, which is why a qualified representative should be involved.

Clients defer to age 85 when they don't need the money, and withdrawing it will cause an unnecessary taxation. The QLAC reduces the RMD each year during the deferral period and the tax due on that distribution. The RMD is reduced because the QLAC allows for the deferral of the taxation. It is the first time in the history that the IRS is allowing an exception to the RMD rule.

In a nutshell,

- The deferred amount can only be put into fixed annuities.

- The deferral period can be any number of years up to age 85.

- Income from the QLAC must start no later than the first of the month after your 85th birthday.

- Payments must be in the form of "life only" or "life with cash refund" annuity payments. The "life only" option pays out a larger monthly payout, but once you die, the income stops. This isn't a good option for anyone with a partner since the account is now closed and finished. Choosing "life with cash refund" ensures money continues to your loved one after your death.

- The maximum amount is indexed for inflation annually by the IRS—meaning the return is guaranteed to be higher than the rate of inflation if held to maturity. This is a risk-free, guaranteed return.

Unless you have no heirs, you should never take the income only, or life only option. You get significantly more monthly income, but in Mable's case, her daughter would've gotten nothing. Selecting options is a critical decision that you get only one chance to do. Once you select these options they're irrevocable. Even with the choice of your beneficiary. Botton line—once selected, you can't change your mind.

What exactly is a QLAC?

A QLAC is nothing more than a fixed longevity annuity that postpones the RMD until a later time. In simple terms, it is a contract with an insurance company that ensures you will not outlive your money. What you're buying is an income stream, with a guaranteed rate of return.

A longevity annuity is just another type of annuity, except it postpones taking the income stream until some specified time in the future to avoid the risk of running out of money. Since the contract holder has given up the money in exchange for an income stream, there is technically no account value from which to take RMDs, so, none are due at 70.5.

How QLACs Work

One of the unique benefits of the QLAC product is that the monthly payout amount isn't part of your RMD calculation. One of my clients, Peg, a single woman, can meet her bills on her pension alone, yet has money in IRAs that she must withdraw since she is close to 70.5 and ready to retire. She wants some cash on hand to travel, and wants to have a little money to leave behind to her church.

When shopping for the right QLAC for Peg, I researched among a number of different insurance carriers. Each insurance company will determine a different monthly payout, depending on the age you want to receive payments. Four independent agencies—A.M. Best, Fitch, Moody's and Standard & Poor's—rate the financial strength of insurance companies.[26]

---

26 http://www.iii.org/article/how-to-assess-the-financial-strength-of-an-insurance-company

I put $125,000 of her $500,000 IRA asset total into a QLAC, which would give her an income stream at age 85, when she anticipated she might need it. Calculating her RMD using this scenario, the amount would be $375,000 instead of $500,000. The portion of her IRA balance used to buy the QLAC is excluded from the funds used to calculate the RMDs Peg was required to take.

To find the best QLAC for Peg's situation, I examined the differences between monthly payouts among the different insurance companies. Each insurance company has their own tables that they use to determine these monthly payouts. I took the highest payout for Peg, but with the understanding the insurance company rating was among the best in the industry.

Peg, without any heirs, had different needs than my wife's friend Mabel, who had a daughter she wanted to leave a legacy to. Although their reasons for a QLAC were different, both women had two goals that were the same: they wanted their money to outlast them and they wanted to pay as little tax as possible.

QLAC and Medicare Surcharges

In 2017, the Medicare tables for individuals and married couples are being lowered while the surcharges are being increased.[27] What you pay will be based on Medicare's income calculation, not on your 1040. If you go $1 over that stated amount, you will be hit with the full surcharge.

Full surcharges are income calculations done by the Social Security Administration every 2 years starting at age 63 when a surcharge of 30-90% is applied to income earners in excess of certain earnings. Social Security is not the income stream for senior citizens it once was, as Medicare payments and Medicare surcharges are deducted right off the top.

Even if you need to take your RMD because you need it to live, it's sometimes a good idea to do a little QLAC to lower your income. This way, you can defer some of that money and lower the Medicare B and

---

27 https://www.federalregister.gov/articles/2015/04/15/2015-08514/medicare-and-medicaid-programs-electronic-health-record-incentive-program-modifications-to

D surcharges. The QLAC defers the RMD which causes a taxable event not to occur which in turn forces your income down and avoids the surcharge of Part B and Part D of Medicare.

Remember, it's not about what you make, it's about what you keep. It's important for the person buying the QLAC (and the beneficiary) to fully understand the details of Medicare surcharges to make an informed decision regarding the RMD. Of course, if you need the money, you can use it—you'll just be taxed on the portion you use. But there are ways to keep taxes at a minimum, and QLACs are a perfect scenario for continued savings, avoiding taxes and passing money on to heirs.

Mabel versus Peg

Mabel's only beneficiary, her daughter Kate, could have ended up with a minimum of a 28 percent tax on whatever lump sum she received after her mother's death, had she not planned. Granted, Kate may have desperately needed the money, and that could be accounted for in an emergency. But in a meeting with Mable and Kate, their concerns were tax-deferred, long-term savings.

Unforeseen circumstances had Peg actually needing more of her income at the time she was doing her RMD. But once we factored in Medicare Part B and D surcharges, we discovered she was better off taking less of her RMD as cash, as that would've changed her tax situation. Both Peg and Mabel needed QLACs for different reasons, and setup to achieve different results.

By Peg taking the maximum $125,000 QLAC, it in turn lowered her Medicare B and Medicare D surcharges. That structure ended up giving her more money each month than if she had taken more of the RMD to live on. Taking more of a withdrawal and putting less into a QLAC would've upped her income, and pushed her into a higher tax bracket and surcharge situation.

The income is deferred, which lowers your tax that year. You're in a way delaying your taxes due, but are also creating a secondary pension plan since people are living much longer.

Mable, on the other hand, had more than enough income to live on and her biggest concern was keeping the money for a later income stream if need be, and setup a legacy for Kate, something that would only be touched in an emergency. Hopefully, it would be something that Kate would pass on to her own children some day. Which brings us to the stretch IRA.

Stretch– It's a concept, not a product

The term "stretch" IRA is not a type of Individual Retirement Account, but rather it is a feature used in estate planning or a financial strategy that allows people to stretch out the life—and therefore the tax advantages—of an IRA.[28] It's used to avoid both RMDs by the original IRA owner, and defer taxes. In effect, someone dies and leaves his IRA to someone other than his spouse. The beneficiary—even if it's a child—inherits the IRA tax benefits as well, and can keep the money in the account and not pay taxes until it is withdrawn at retirement age. It's basically assigning a beneficiary to your IRA that's not a spouse.

That's a great benefit for anyone who knows they won't need their retirement funds at all, and doesn't want to be forced into a RMD and tax situation. Another benefit is that the IRA also can be passed on from generation to generation while beneficiaries enjoy tax-deferred growth as long as possible. The stretch IRA concept is something Congress tries to modify often, and there is always political chatter that the rules will change.[29] A stretch strategy,

- Offers your heirs the potential for decades of tax-advantaged growth.

- Is an effective tool to transfer wealth and build a legacy.

- Extends the benefits of tax-deferred growth potential into future generations.

---

28 http://www.investopedia.com/terms/s/stretch-ira.asp

29 http://www.cnbc.com/2015/03/02/obama-2016-budget-would-end-the-stretch-ira.html

- Can provide heirs with an annual stream of supplementary income.

For Mabel, the stretch IRA was a secondary measure aside from the QLAC in order to provide a legacy for her daughter Kate. Working with Kate on her own financial planning, the goal was for that particular IRA to grow with as much tax-deferred money as possible, for three generations, the maximum allowable by the IRS.

To understand it further, consider if Mabel suddenly died and Kate became the immediate owner of the IRA. According to the IRS life-expectancy tables, Kate is expected to live another 43.6 years, so her RMD in the first year is approximately $7,400 ($300,000 times 8% growth, divided by 43.6). This means about $2,100 would be due in taxes.

By the end of the first five years, Kate postponed paying more than $94,000 in taxes, allowing the IRA money to grow tax deferred. As long as Kate takes just RMD each year, her IRA will grow to nearly $900,000 by age 65.

It's important to name a beneficiary to an IRA if it's not your intention to use the money for retirement. There's particular paper work involved and all the right steps must be followed to make sure your beneficiaries take full advantage of a stretch IRA.

Summary

QLACS

- Roth IRAs can't be considered for QLACs.

- For traditional IRAs, the 25 percent limit is based on the ending balance of all traditional IRAs owned by the consumer, including SEP and SIMPLE IRAs, as of December 31 of the year prior to the year that the QLAC is purchased. The fair market value of a QLAC held in an IRA will also be included in that total, even though it won't be for RMD purposes.

- These new retirement tools can reduce RMDs, fill potential income gaps and limit retirees' tax liabilities.

- The 25 percent limit is applied in a slightly different manner to 401(k)s and similar plans. For starters, the 25 percent limit is applied separately to each plan balance. In addition, instead of applying the 25 percent limit to the prior year-end balance of the plan, the 25 percent limit is applied to the balance on the last valuation date. Then, that balance is further adjusted by adding in contributions made between the last valuation and the time the QLAC premium is made, and by subtracting from that balance distributions made during the same time frame.

- In addition to the 25 percent limits described above, there is also a $125,000 limit on total QLAC purchases by a client. When looked at in concert with the 25 percent limit, the $125,000 limit becomes a "lesser of" rule. In other words, a client can invest no more than the lesser of 25 percent of retirement funds or $125,000 in QLACs.

Stretch IRA

- A stretch IRA is a distribution strategy for the inheritors of IRA accounts.

- If you take the simple step of naming beneficiaries to your retirement account, those beneficiaries can choose to stretch the distributions over their life expectancies. That could save them significant amounts of taxes and enable them to grow the balance further on a tax-deferred basis.

- The stretch strategy works because of the tax-advantaged feature of an IRA account; investments inside an IRA account increase in value without any immediate tax consequences.

- Per the stretch strategy, the IRA account—and its remaining account balance after any IRS-mandated required minimum distributions (RMD)—is passed from beneficiary to beneficiary. Each time the account moves to a younger beneficiary, the amount of the RMD decreases. This is because younger individuals are subject to smaller RMDs than older individuals (due a younger individual's longer life longevity).

- A stretch strategy is most effective when an IRA is passed not to a child, but a grandchild, or even a great grandchild. Each generation skipped means smaller RMDs, which means a larger balance of the IRA account can grow tax-advantaged. This equates to more value for heirs.

- This concept allows the IRA investments to continue to grow tax deferred even after the death of the original account owner. This is a way for a taxpayer to leave his or her IRA to younger generation beneficiaries and defer the taxation of the untaxed profits inside the IRA as long as possible.

Increasing Your Social Security Benefit While Lowering Your Taxes

Jeff Klauenberg, MA, CIS, CFP®
Will Heil, CPA/PFS, CFP®

One very common dilemma for people approaching retirement is trying to figure out the best date for starting to take their Social Security distributions. The current rules give you an eight-year window to start receiving your benefits. You can start taking Social Security when you turn sixty-two and you can delay all the way until you turn seventy. Here's the kicker, your Social Security retirement benefits increase dramatically for each year that you postpone receiving them.

Social Security Claiming Methods

We can go ahead and make a general assumption at the outset of considering these questions relating to issues and solutions regarding Social Security benefits distribution: it can get pretty complicated. Much like IRS rules and regulations, there are tiers of interrelated factors that can influence your decision and there are a variety of methods for claiming your benefits. You can claim them early yet delay distribution, which can significantly enhance benefits, if you are married. For a couple that has reached full retirement age and are still working, this can be a very productive tactic. Also, much like the taxes, these rules and regulations are like a moving target, constantly at the mercy of congress. As a glaring example, as this chapter and book were about ready to be printed, the rules were changed without warning.

On November 2, 2015, the Bipartisan Budget Act of 2015 was signed into law by President Barack Obama. This budget agreement raised the debt ceiling, thereby funding the government through March 15, 2017. In doing so, the agreement eliminated the two sophisticated social security claiming strategies that are explained in this chapter: file-and-suspend and file-a-restricted-claim.

These two strategies are still viable for millions of retiring Americans. The new qualification to use the strategies is that the spouse who is going to "file-and-suspend" must be FRA of 66 and must "file-and-suspend" before 180 days after November 2, 2015. Also, the spouse who will be "filing-a-restricted-claim" for spousal benefits only, has to be at least 62 by December 31, 2015.

Since millions of retirees will qualify, I will keep the original discussion and example. BUT, remember the clock is ticking and will run out 180 days from November 2, 2015 which by my calculations will be April 30, 2016 (the Social Security Administration will direct the enactment of these provisions and will determine final effective dates).

For all others the new rule basically eliminates the ability to receive a spousal benefit while both spouses suspend their own benefit. The following discussion and example will also address the loss of this spousal benefit.

The "File and Suspend" rule was enacted in the year 2000 as part of the Senior Citizens' Freedom to Work Act. Sticking with our "it can get pretty complicated" theme, the rule states that a spouse can File and Suspend in regards to his or her own benefit and submit a Restricted Application for spousal benefits. This allows their own benefit to keep growing at around 8% per year. Don't worry; there are some "pretty complicated" calculation tables to substantiate these claims. Combining the File and Suspend Rule with the Restricted Application can be an excellent way to receive some of a couple's benefits while allowing other benefits to increase with time.

Done correctly, these steps can mean a difference of hundreds of dollars per month or more for a retiring couple. If these filings are not performed according to particular rules, in correct order and respecting certain dates, you stand to lose significant benefits. The "Claim Now, Claim More Later" strategy is similar and can provide for a couple to receive some benefits earlier while allowing other benefits to grow until they elect to claim them at a later date.

One thing these claiming methods have in common is that they take advantage of one of Social Security's major features—your monthly benefit increases when you wait to collect. Collecting before "Full Retirement Age" (FRA) cuts your benefit drastically. FRA is age 66 for those born 1943-54, and increases gradually to 67 for those born 1960 or later. Postponing beyond your FRA will increase your Social Security benefit 8% each year until age 70, plus a cost-of-living-adjustment (COLA). Considering current average returns for safety-focused growth funds is closer to 3%, the guaranteed 8% annual growth plus COLA allowance is an attractive investment and should be seriously considered.

Each claiming method has its own strengths and weaknesses, so your particular situation may favor one or another. Life expectancy, for example, can change the results of each. "How is your health?" That's an important question that we ask our clients, because if their health is poor, especially if their ancestors didn't live long, we will recommend taking Social Security sooner. Waiting for a higher monthly benefit does not make sense if you are not around long enough to receive the increased monthly payments.

To better understand these claiming methods, let's talk about a couple that we have been working with since they were 61 years old. Rob and Nicole had originally planned to apply for their Social Security benefits at age 62. If they had decided to start drawing at 62, their benefits would have been only $1,875 for Rob and $1,500 for Nicole. Assuming that Rob lives to age 86, Nicole lives to age 92, and inflation averages 2.5% during their retirement, they would collect combined cumulative lifetime benefits of $1,596,087.

Since they were both still working, we ran a social security analysis and showed them the advantage of waiting at least until they were at FRA of 66.

By waiting until their FRA age of 66 to claim their Social Security benefits, Rob and Nicole are rewarded with a higher benefit for life. Now they can collect $2,500 and $2,000 per month respectively, which is a monthly increase of 33% and will total $1,693,424. If they were able to wait until age 70 (after which there are no more benefit increases), their respective monthly benefits would increase to $3,462 and $2,914, totaling $1,939,328 over their lifetimes. Delaying receipt of benefits for eight years could result in over $300,000 of increased retirement income. Regardless of how complicated the rules may be, a quarter of a million dollars is a significant benefit to not overlook.

Rob and Nicole are now planning to claim benefits when they retire at age 66, but since both are in good health and expect a full lifespan; we recommended taking advantage of their good health and proposed a better plan for claiming benefits. At age 66 Rob files for Social Security benefits and immediately suspends payments (File and Suspend). This allows his benefit amount to continue growing while at the same time allowing Nicole to claim spousal benefits. When Nicole turns 66 she files an application for benefits that is restricted to spousal benefits (Restricted Application). This lets Nicole's benefit grow while she draws the spousal benefit (50% of Rob's benefit). Nicole continues to draw the spousal benefit until reaching age 70, switching to her own benefit at that time (Claim Now – Claim More Later). Rob begins to draw his benefit at age 70 (Wait to Collect). This is a powerful combination, earning them $2,001,615 in cumulative benefits. (Note: Under new law, they have to apply before April 30, 2016 or will not qualify for spousal benefits.)

Keep in mind that claiming plans could have results that are worse or better than any of the amounts above and that your personal circumstances and life expectancy play a significant role in the ultimate payouts. If all goes as expected for Rob and Nicole, our plan will help them collect $308,191 more Social Security income during retirement than if they claimed benefits at 66, as they had originally planned. The result is that after the 4 years their joint Social Security income at age 70 will increase from $4,500 to $6,376; an increase of 42% for the rest of their lives.

Their question now is, "How do we cover the lost Social Security income?" How do we cover the 4 year gap between age 66 and 70?

What is the Gap?

While these strategies are designed to maximize Social Security over your lifetime, for many people this leaves an income gap between the date of retirement and age 70. The lost income for someone retiring at the full retirement age of 66, with the maximum Social Security benefit in 2014, would be $2,642 per month. This would be a four year total loss, including a 1.9% COLA, of $130,668. There are several solutions that can help bridge that income gap.

Income Base

Before establishing an income replacement plan of action, determine what your basic income needs would be each year during the four year gap period. To determine how much income you need, you have to analyze your expenses. A good place to start is with your necessary expenses—these items do not change much from year to year. After the necessities, you have expenses for the fun things in life—your planned and desired activities and purchases. Some things you can put on hold, some things you might be willing to forgo, others you just do and enjoy. At retirement, you may have a list of discretionary expenses that have been put off, like a new kitchen or new car, the long-awaited vacation, or paying off all your bills. Remember this is only a 4 year period that can significantly increase your future guaranteed income. What we tell recent retirees is to slow down, take a breath, and plan your future. Reducing some expenses during these gap years can pay off handsomely after age 70, but will postponing some spending be enough to "fill the gap?"

For most people there remains a sizeable enough income gap between retirement age and age 70 that other means of income supplementation are required. The first suggestion to fill the gap is often working part time. Although many use part time work as a transition into retirement or to keep busy it may not be the most desirable option. In addition, the earned income could cause a portion of the Social Security benefit to be taxable. It is possible for as much as 85% of your Social Security benefit to be taxable. Approaching these tax thresholds is counter-productive, which means that earned income may not be the best alternative for meeting your needs during the Social Security benefit gap years. This leads us to considering other retirement assets for replacing the lost Social Security benefit before your 70th birthday.

Solutions

The basic strategy for filling the gap is to create a four year ladder using safe liquid investments like certificates of deposit (CD), short-term individual bonds, short-term bond funds or exchange-traded bond funds (ETFs), as well as a savings account. As an example, a savings account, a one-year CD, a two-year CD, and a short-term bond ETF could be used. The savings account would be funded with the first year's "income gap" amount. The one and two-year CDs would be funded with the gap amounts that will be needed for the second and third years, respectively. If you estimated your gap correctly, the savings account will be drawn down to near zero by the end of your first year of retirement. For each of the following years the savings account would be replenished annually first with transfers from the one year CD, then the two year CD, and finally from the short-term bond ETF. This is a very conservative approach, so the results can be counted on with a high degree of certainty. One potential negative is that current interest rates are very low, although this could change in the future. Also, if interest rates rise, the value of the bond ETF may decrease. As always, it is imperative to consider the tax implications of the investment.

Another conservative solution would be to use a 5-year immediate annuity. A benefit of this approach is that you would know exactly what the monthly income would be, and that payout is guaranteed. One drawback is that you have given up ownership of the principal and may only be able to get it back over the 5 year guarantee period. If you die, you may not get your remaining principal back at all, depending on the annuity's design. One advantage of using a non-qualified immediate annuity is the "Exclusion Ratio". For every withdrawal, part of the income is a return of principal and therefore not taxable.

You can setup a monthly, quarterly, or annual systematic withdrawal from your retirement accounts (like your IRA, 401(k) or 403(b)). The best way to do this would be to open a side IRA account and transfer enough principal to cover the four years. This fund should be invested in a similar fashion as the 4 year ladder described above. Then each month or quarter, a withdrawal would be transferred to your savings account.

The above ideas can help people who waited until they were near retirement to do their Social Security planning. The earlier you start planning the more solutions that are available to you. One strategy for early planners is to create a bond ladder of zero-coupon, tax-free municipal bonds that are staggered to mature on a regular basis throughout the 4 years of delayed Social Security benefits. Zero-coupon municipal bonds are long-term investments that are purchased at a deep discount, paying out tax-free interest only once, at maturity.

Another strategy would be to start contributing to a Roth 401 (k) or IRA. Although you will not be able to deduct the contribution off your taxes, the income will be tax-free in retirement (after the 5 year qualifying period).

Tax Impacts

Income to fund the 4 year gap will come from either a taxable, tax-deferred, or tax-exempt account. With all strategies, the funding will eventually end up in a one year liquid account. For our purposes, I will call it a savings account.

If the money comes from a taxable account (also called "non-qualified" or "previously taxed") like a bank CD or investment taxable bonds, the principal would have already been taxed. The current interest, dividends, and capital gains, both short-term and long-term, will be taxed as realized. Interest and short-term capital gains will be taxed as ordinary income and dividends and long-term capital gains will be taxed between 0% and 20% depending on your tax bracket.

With tax-deferred accounts (called "tax-qualified" or "retirement accounts"), the contributions and growth have not been taxed. Therefore, 100% of the distributions will be taxed. Also, the total yearly distributions may bump you up into a higher tax bracket.

Tax-exempt accounts (Municipal bonds, Roth IRAs and Life Insurance Cash Value) will not generate Federal tax and possibly not State taxes. However, municipal bond interest will be considered in the calculation to determine the percent of your Social Security benefit that will be taxed.

Order of Withdrawal

Typical tax planning "liquidation strategy" says that we should draw from taxable accounts first. Next would be tax-qualified accounts (401ks, 403b, IRA) or tax-exempt account (Roth accounts, Life Insurance Cash Value) in order to extend the deferral on the earnings as long as possible. The order of tax-deferred or tax-exempt will depend on your outlook for taxes. If you believe your taxes will increase in the future, tax-deferred would take priority. This will allow the tax-exempt assets to grow and when taxes are higher, the tax-exempt interest will have a greater effect. If your view is that your taxes will be lower, taking tax-exempt first would be more favorable, giving you lower taxes today.

During the four year gap you can take a more active strategy and focus on reducing the tax liability of the income generated. There are two areas of tax to manage, staying within your current tax-bracket and possibly a lower bracket, and reducing the percent of Social Security benefits taxed.

Social Security Benefit Tax

(Note: New law eliminated spousal benefit while suspending own benefit beginning 4/30/16)

If during the 4 year gap to age 70 you decide to take the spousal benefit, you should calculate the amount of that benefit that would be taxed. For couples whose sum of their adjustable gross income, nontaxable interest and half of the spousal Social Security benefit is lower than $32,000, they will not have to pay income tax on that benefit. For benefits greater than $32,000, they will pay tax on an increasing percentage of that spousal benefit until it reaches 50% at $44,000. From this point on, 85% of the benefit may be taxed. Sources that will make your benefit taxable are work, interest, dividends, taxable pension payments, traditional qualified retirement plans, IRAs, and tax-exempt interest from municipal bonds and U.S. savings bonds.

What are not considered in the calculation are Roth IRA accounts and Life Insurance cash value withdrawals. Also, if you receive only Social Security, even if it is more than the $32,000 and $44,000, your benefit is not taxed until one – half of the benefit equals $32,000 or $44,000 ($64,000 and $88,000 total joint benefit).

Tax Bracket Considerations

There are 7 tax brackets as of 2015.[1] Since my example is of a couple using the spousal benefit, I will show only married couples filing jointly. Bracket 1 is taxable income up to $18,450 (tax rate of 10%), bracket 2 $18,450 - $74,900 (15%), bracket 3 would be $74,900 - $151,200 (25%), bracket 4 $151,200 - $230,450 (28%), bracket 5 $230,450 - $411,500 (33%), bracket 6 $411,500 - $413,200 (35%), and over $413,200 (39.6%).

The choice of taxable, tax-deferred, or tax-exempt assets and the mix of these assets will help supply the needed income while lowering the tax ramifications. The procedure that we use is to first calculate for the minimum percentage of Social Security benefit that will be taxed. Then we work on the lowest Income Tax bracket.

Putting it All Together

To maximize the Social Security benefit, the process should start with an analysis of your expenses to define your "necessary" and "discretionary" expenses. The goal is to identify the bottom-line with which you are comfortable. The next step is to calculate the income needed to cover that bottom-line of expenses starting with the spousal Social Security benefit. The difference between the spousal benefit and the income needed is the "gap" that needs to be filled with part-time work and/or your assets. The type of assets used to generate the income, whether it is taxable, tax-deferred, or tax-exempt, will depend on the tax bracket and Social Security tax threshold you target.

Putting the Numbers Together

Let's revisit Rob and Nicole so that we can better understand which accounts to withdraw from during the gap. For our claiming plan to work, they need to replace the monthly benefits that they decided to forgo during the gap period. So, how much Social Security do they need to replace?

Their original plan was to fund $80,000 of expenses with their current Social Security monthly benefits which they calculated as $54,000 annually ($2,500 + $2,000 = $4,500 total, times 12 months). They were planning on withdrawing $26,000 from Rob's Traditional IRA. This plan of action would have resulted in 25% of the spousal Social Security benefit being taxed as well as the $26,000 from the IRA.

An analysis of the expenses showed that their "Necessary" expenses were $60,000 and their "Discretionary" was $20,000. The Discretionary expenses for the 4 years were trips of $10,000 each year and home repairs also totaling $10,000.

Maximizing Social Security Benefits

Our plan was to maximize their Social Security benefits and reduce their taxes. To do this we needed to first replace the $54,000 of postponed Social Security benefit. We started with the spousal benefit that Nicole would receive. This will cut that lost income by $1,250 per month, that's $15,000 annually. After we discussed their net gap of $39,000, Nicole decided to take advantage of an offer to work part-time for her previous employer for about $1,000 per month, which lowers their annual gap by $12,000 to $27,000. Over the four years between ages 66 and 70, including a 2.5% COLA (a cost-of-living adjustment calculation we use in long-term income planning), the $27,000 would be a net loss of income of $112,118.

To fund the gap, they will need to draw from their accounts. They have joint taxable accounts of $50,000 in the bank and $100,000 in brokerage accounts. Both Rob and Nicole have Traditional IRA balances of $569,178 each and Roth IRA balances of $150,000 each. They also own four $6,050 joint Zero-Coupon Tax-Free Municipal Bonds, one maturing each of the four years from 66-70. They each also have $75,000 Cash Value in their Life Insurance. Their total portfolio assets available for retirement are therefore $1,758,356. Neither of them have a pension to help fill the gap.

The Four Year Solution

Below I am going to map out a four year solution for Rob and Nicole. While this solution can work in real life, it has been created as an example to illustrate what can be done and why. It is also based on current 2015 investment and tax code.

Following this 4 year example I will run another 4 year example using the new Social Security rules.

Now let's see how Rob and Nicole through tax and financial planning can stay in the lowest tax bracket while receiving the highest Social Security benefits and income. Please follow tables 1-3 for calculations.

The Starting Line - Years 1 and 2- Ages 66 and 67 - Table 1

1) Expenses

Rob and Nicole had agreed to try and keep their expenses at the necessary level of $60,000.

2) Spousal Social Security Benefit

Since Nicole is going to receive a spousal benefit of $15,000 a year, the first step was to calculate what the maximum taxable income would be to keep her benefit from being taxed. As stated earlier, the percent of Social Security benefit taxed is based on the taxable income (AGI), plus non-taxable interest and half of the Social Security. Our calculations started with the minimum threshold of $32,000, we then subtracted half of Nicole's benefit, which was $7,500, (one half of the $15,000), the result was $24,500 of qualified taxable income.

3) Minimum Federal Tax Bracket

The next step took the taxable Social Security threshold income of $24,500 and subtracted the maximum Federal taxable income to stay in the lowest tax bracket of 10%, $18,450. The result is an excess income of $6,050 that needed to be eliminated as taxable income in order to stay in the 10% bracket.

4) Reduction of Excess AGI

By using the zero-coupon municipal bond to fund the $6,050, we would keep the taxable income at the 10% bracket. With the addition of Nicole's part time work of $12,000 and a $6,450 distribution from the traditional IRAs, we are able to generate $24,500 in income and stay in the 10% Federal tax bracket. Add to this the spousal Social Security benefit of $15,000 and we would have a total income now of $39,500. Our target is $60,000, so we need $20,500 more income. How do we do this and still stay in the 10% Federal tax bracket and not affect Social Security taxation?

5) Non-taxable Income

A non-taxable withdrawal from the Roth IRAs fills the gap while not affecting the Social Security taxation or the Federal tax bracket.

8) Total Income

Their total income is $15,000 from Social Security, $12,000 from part-time work, $20,500 from the Roth IRA, $6,050 from the zero-coupon tax free municipal bond, and $6,450 from the traditional IRA for a total of $60,000. They are really happy to know that they are getting $60,000 in income and only have to pay ZERO federal taxes!

Extra Spending - Years 3 and 4- Ages 68 and 69 Table 2

The first two years worked as well as we had planned. Rob and Nicole were happy with the income and low taxes. They also found that they were still able to do most of what they wanted. The sacrifice was only in "big ticket" wants. But by the third year they were getting restless and wanted to take a trip that would cost them $10,000 and their house needed some repairs that would cost another $10,000. They decided to first do the needed repairs and then in year 4 take their dream trip. The challenge they now faced was how to fund the extra expenses and maintain their low tax bracket? We went back to our calculations on table 2.

As you can see, we were able to keep everything the same. Each year the extra $10,000 that was needed, for their repairs and trip, came from their life insurance cash value. We made an analysis of their two life insurance policies and found that since Rob and Nicole had been over-funding their policies for years they could withdraw $10,000 from each and it did not affect the projected longevity of the policies.

Rob and Nicole were pleased that they could do this withdrawal and were thrilled that it was considered a tax-free withdrawal. They were still in the lowest 10% Federal tax bracket.

The Goal Line - Year 5 - Age 70 - Table 3

Rob and Nicole have made it to age 70. Now they are both receiving the maximum Social Security payment. Instead of the $54,000 they would have received at the Full Retirement Age of 66, they are now receiving $76,512 per year and this will increase with Social Security Cost-of-Living increases. With patience, solid planning and analysis and a little sacrifice, they realized an annual income that is $26,512 greater than if they had started Social Security earlier. They were also able to accomplish this while paying the least amount in Federal taxes. That feat is unfortunately no longer possible.

Now that Rob and Nicole are 70 years old, they will be forced to start withdrawing Required Minimum Distributions (70.5) from their traditional IRAs. Since they have withdrawn very little from these IRAs, their values have grown. At just 5% growth the account values could be over $1,300,000. This would generate a RMD in the first year of approximately $50,000. This added to the Social Security of $76,512 will total $126,512 in income. Now, up to 85% of their $76,512 Social Security and all of the IRA RMD of $50,000 will be taxed resulting in a taxable income of $93,618.

Effects of New Social Security Law

As stated earlier, the primary effect of the new law is to eliminate the ability to draw a spousal benefit while suspending their own benefits and thereby increasing their Social Security benefits. The spousal benefit in the example was $15,000 per year and remained tax-free by staying within the income guidelines. To make our example work under the new law, we now have to come up with a new plan.

As Table 4 shows, for years 1 and 2 Nicole's salary of $12,000 and a $6,450 distribution from the IRAs keeps their taxable income within the 10% Federal tax bracket of $18,450. The rest of the $41,550 income needed will come from a $6,050 tax-free zero-coupon municipal bond, $10,000 distribution from the brokerage account which is considered cost-basis, and $25,500 from the tax-free Roth IRAs. Total income is $60,000 with only $18,450 taxable.

In Table 5, to stay within the 10% bracket and cover the additional $10,000 of discretionary expenses, $10,000 is withdrawn from their life insurance cash values, a non-taxable event, and $35,500 from their Roth IRAs.

Table 6 shows that the new law does not affect their Social Security or their income after age 70.

The Future

Who knows what the future may bring. We just saw that the IRS or Congress may change Social Security rules, and in the future may change our tax rates and/or alter the structure and effects of allowed deductions and exemptions. Investments may change as well as interest rates. Rob and Nicole are off to a good start. They have more assets in their Roth IRA and Life Insurance Cash Values to help offset future taxes. If their tax rate does increase, they know that they are starting off at the lowest level they could. They also know that their planning gave them the highest Social Security benefits that they could receive.

One takeaway from Rob and Nicole's example is that the planning needed to start years before they decided to retire. The Roth IRA, zero-coupon municipal bond, and life insurance cash value needed to be started at least ten years before retirement in order to be available for the tax-free income needed to keep their taxable income within the 10% Federal tax bracket.

There are few easy answers when it comes to combining multiple tactics, products, instruments, needs, desires and contingencies to arrive at an overall strategy that satisfies your retirement income demands. However, our complex systems of taxation and guaranteed benefit distributions do allow for creative solutions to specific challenges such as maximizing Social Security benefit income and providing tax-advantaged income in the resulting gap years. The process can be arduous, the details can get mind numbing, but the results can be enormously rewarding and often life changing. Attack the situation head on with your advisers close-at-hand and you may be surprised at how much you can accomplish and benefit in your retirement years.

Table 1
Years 1 & 2 – Ages 66 – 67
Necessary Expenses = $60,000

			Sources of Income	Income minus Expenses
1	Calculate Expenses			Expenses $60,000
2	Calculate Max Income for Tax-Free Spousal Social Security	Max AGI + Tax-Exempt Interest $32,000 ½ Social Security $7,500 Max Taxable Income $24,500		
3	Max 10% Federal Tax Bracket Taxable Income	Max Step 2 Taxable Income $24,500 10% Fed Tax Bracket $18,450 Excess Fed Taxable Income $6,050	Part-time Work $12,000 Traditional IRA $6,450	
4	Reduction of Fed Taxable Income	Excess Fed Taxable Income $6,050 -Municipal Tax-Exempt Bond $6,050 Excess Taxable Income $0.00	Tax-Exempt Munl Bond $6,050	
5	Add Tax-Free Social Security		Tax-Free Social Security $15,000	
6	Non-Taxable Income		Roth IRA $20,500	Total Income $60,000
7	Taxable Income			Taxable Income $18,450
8	Total Taxes	$0.00 = 0% effective Tax Rate		

Table 2
Years 3 & 4 – Ages 68 – 69
Necessary Expenses + Discretionary = $70,000

			Sources of Income	Income minus Expenses
1	Calculate Expenses			Expenses $70,000
2	Calculate Max Income for Tax-Free Social Security	Max AGI + Tax-Exempt Interest $32,000 ½ Social Security $7,500 Max Taxable Income $24,500		
3	Max 10% Federal Tax Bracket Taxable Income	Max Step 2 Taxable Income $24,500 10% Fed Tax Bracket $18,450 Excess Fed Taxable Income $6,050	Part-time Work $12,000 Traditional IRA $6,450	
4	Reduction of Fed Taxable Income	Excess Fed Taxable Income $6,050 -Municipal Tax-Exempt Bond $6,050 Excess Taxable Income $0.00	Tax-Exempt Munl Bond $6,050	
5	Add Tax-Free Social Security		Tax-Free Social Security $15,000	
6	Non-Taxable Income		Roth IRA $20,500 Life Insurance Cash Value $10,000	
7	Total Income - Expenses			Total Income $70,000 Total Expenses $70,000
8	Taxable Income			Taxable Income $18,450
9	Total Taxes	$0.00 = 0% effective Tax Rate		

Table 3
Years 5 – Age 70
Necessary Expenses + Discretionary = $80,000

			Sources of Income	Income minus Expenses
1	Calculate Expenses			Expenses $80,000
2	Calculate Max Income for Tax-Free Social Security	Max AGI + Tax-Exempt Interest $32,000 ½ Social Security $38,256 Max Taxable Income (over) $6,256		
3	Reduce Excess Taxable Income	($50,000 RMD + $38,256 ½ Social Security = $88,256) (up to 85% of social security now taxed = $43,618)		
4	Max 10% Federal Tax Bracket Taxable Income	Max Step 3 Taxable Income $0.00 10% Fed Tax Bracket $18,450 Excess Fed Taxable Income $0.00	Traditional IRA RMD $50,000	
5	Add Social Security		Social Security $76,512	
6	Non-Taxable Income		0.00	
7	Total Income - Expenses			Total Income $126,512 Total Expenses $80,000
7	Taxable Income			Taxable Income $93,618
8	Total Taxes	$9,655 = 7.63% effective Tax Rate		

Table 4
Years 1 & 2 – Ages 66 – 67
Necessary Expenses = $60,000

			Sources of Income	Income minus Expenses
1	Calculate Expenses			Expenses $60,000
2	Calculate Max Income for Tax-Free Spousal Social Security	Nov 2, 2015 Bipartisan Budget Act eliminates Spousal Social Security		
3	Max 10% Federal Tax Bracket Taxable Income	10% Fed Tax Bracket $18,450	Part-time Work $12,000 Traditional IRA $6,450	
4	Tax-Exempt Income	Municipal Tax-Exempt Bond	Tax-Exempt Munl Bond $6,050	
5	Non-Taxable Income	Brokerage Account cost-basis Roth IRA	Brokerage cost-basis $10,000 Roth IRA $25,500	
6	Total Income - Expenses			Total Income $60,000 Total Expenses $60,000
7	Taxable Income			Taxable Income $18,450
8	Total Taxes	$0.00 = 0% effective Tax Rate		

Table 5
Years 3 & 4 – Ages 68 – 69
Necessary + Discretionary Expenses = $70,000

			Sources of Income	Income minus Expenses
1	Calculate Expenses			Expenses $70,000
2	Calculate Max Income for Tax-Free Spousal Social Security	Nov 2, 2015 Bipartisan Budget Act eliminates Spousal Social Security		
3	Max 10% Federal Tax Bracket Taxable Income	10% Fed Tax Bracket $18,450	Part-time Work $12,000 Traditional IRA $6,450	
4	Tax-Exempt Income		Muni $6,050	
5	Non-Taxable Income	Roth IRA Life Insurance Cash Value	Roth IRA $35,500 Life Ins Cash Value $10,000	
6	Total Income - Expenses			Total Income $70,000 Total Expenses $70,000
7	Taxable Income			Taxable Income $18,450
8	Total Taxes	$1,845 = 2.9% effective Tax Rate		

Table 6
Years 5 – Age 70
Necessary Expenses + Discretionary = $80,000

			Sources of Income	Income minus Expenses
1	Calculate Expenses			Expenses $80,000
2	Calculate Max Income for Tax-Free Social Security	Max AGI + Tax-Exempt Interest $32,000 ½ Social Security $38,256 Max Taxable Income (over) $6,256		
3	Reduce Excess Taxable Income	($50,000 RMD + $38,256 ½ Social Security = $88,256) (up to 85% of social security now taxed = $43,618)		
4	Max 10% Federal Tax Bracket Taxable Income	Max Step 3 Taxable Income $0.00 10% Fed Tax Bracket $18,450 Excess Fed Taxable Income $0.00	Traditional IRA RMD $50,000	
5	Add Social Security		Social Security $76,512	
6	Non-Taxable Income		0.00	
7	Total Income - Expenses			Total Income $126,512 Total Expenses $80,000
7	Taxable Income			Taxable Income $93,618
8	Total Taxes	$9,655 = 7.63% effective Tax Rate		

*Not affiliated with the Social Security Administration, or any other state or federal government entity. This material does not constitute specific personal tax or investment advice and you are encouraged to consult a professional advisors on such matters.

Section Five:
Implications of Healthcare

How Health Care Cost Impacts Retirement Planning

Michael Tove Ph.D., CEP, RFC

Most retirement planners, and retirement plans, focus on replacing earned income in retirement. Often, planners start with an estimate of the total retirement income based on projected income and expenses, adjust for inflation, calculate the amount of income expected from Social Security and pension benefits and create an income plan to cover any shortfall between what is expected and what is needed. On paper, it all seems clean and tidy, and for a while it may actually work that way. Then, life throws a curve ball and suddenly that "perfect plan" isn't so perfect at all.

The "curve ball" is healthcare costs. Unfortunately, too many people don't include this in their planning, yet the Nationwide Retirement Institute ranks it as the second largest household expense in retirement. Moreover, a Fidelity Investments study (*How to tame retiree health care costs*, 6/11/2014; https://www.fidelity.com/viewpoints/retirement/health-care-costs-when-you-retire), estimates an average 65 year-old will need $220,000 to cover health care costs in retirement. That's not counting increases due to inflation.

For the most part, unexpected health care costs arise from three separate sources:

1. Unanticipated medical insurance premiums.

2. Uninsured medical expenses.
3. Long Term Care.

1. Medical Insurance Costs:

When workers receive medical insurance as a benefit package of their employment, they're insulated from the reality of the insurance premiums and are often shocked at how much the actual cost of health care can be, nor do they fully appreciate how fast it has risen over the past twenty years. For example, the NY Times (Sept. 22, 2014; http://www.nytimes.com/2014/09/23/upshot/in-context-health-premium-increases-dont-actually-look-like-increases.html?_r=0) reported an 8.4% average annual increase in health care premiums, significantly down from pre-Affordable Health Care increases of 9.9% in 2008, 10.8% in 2009 and 11.7% in 2010. However, even at 8.4% annual increase, a major medical plan that cost a family just $350 per month in 1995, would cost $1757 per month in 2015 and by 2020, would be $2629/month.

Most retirees are further held at arm's length from these costs because they don't retire until after age 65 when they are covered by Medicare. Started in 1966, Medicare is a national health plan administered by the Social Security Administration that provides all eligible citizens 65 and older, with medical coverage. Compared with private health insurance, it is relatively inexpensive but doesn't provide complete coverage, and depending on individual circumstances, can become increasingly expensive without warning.

In its current form, Medicare includes four parts:

Medicare Part A (as of 2015): Covers 100% of qualified in-patient hospital care after you pay scheduled deductibles and co-pays as follows:

Days 1-60	$1260 per benefit period deductible
Days 61-90	$315 daily co-pay
Days 91-150	$630 daily co-pay
After 150 days (lifetime)	you pay 100%

Part A does NOT cover out-patient or "Under Observation" facility charges including stays in the ER.

Medicare Part B: Covers charges by doctors, health care providers, preventive benefits, durable medical equipment and out-patient services (including the ER) but only at 80% after you pay a deductible of $147. In addition, Medicare Part B charges a premium, per person, based on how you file and the Adjusted Gross Income (AGI) on your 1040 tax return as follows:

Monthly Premium	File Single	File Joint
$104.90	$85,000 or less	$170,000 or less
$146.90	$85,001–$107,000	$171,001–$214,000
$209.80	$107,001–$160,000	$214,001–$320,000
$272.70	$160,001–$214,000	$320,001–$428,000
$335.70	over $214,000	over $428,000

Medicare Part D (Prescription Drugs) pays for most prescription drugs after you pay a co-pay according to 4 tiers of coverage:

Tier 1 Generic

Tier 2 Preferred Name Brand

Tier 3 Non-preferred Name Brand

Tier 4 Specialty Tier Drugs

The amount of the copay varies from tier-to-tier and plan-to-plan but successively increases with advancing tiers. Most Part D Plans also require a monthly premium that varies by plan but averages $38 per person per month. Like Medicare Part B, the premiums can rise based on filing status and AGI.

Additional Premium	File Single	File Joint
$0	$85,000 or less	$170,000 or less
$12.10	$85,001–$107,000	$171,001–$214,000
$31.10	$107,001–$160,000	$214,001–$320,000
$50.20	$160,001–$214,000	$320,001–$428,000
$69.30	over $214,000	over $428,000

Medicare Supplement (Medigap) Plans are private insurance plans designed to fill in the gaps in traditional Medicare coverage. There are several national standardized plans, each with varying degrees of coverage for different premium amounts. But, for the most popular plan, the average cost for a 65 year-old is around $186/month (Nationwide Retirement Institute, 2015; https://ssc.nwservicecenter.com/media/pdf/NFM-9558M1.pdf); more if you use tobacco. Finally, the monthly premium amount can and frequently does increase in future years with advancing age.

Medicare Part C (Medicare Advantage) Plans: These are privatized plans designed to substitute for Medicare Parts A and B as well as Medicare Supplement. To be eligible for Medicare Advantage, a person must have both Medicare A and B and must continue paying the Part B premium. Otherwise, they can benefit by having everything bundled within a single plan that can be significantly less expensive than Medicare Supplement plans, including in some cases, available at no premium other than Medicare Part B. Moreover, some plans offer what's called a MA-PD plan meaning they automatically include Part D (Prescription Drugs) and in some cases, all that at no cost after the Part B Premium.

However, the trade-off is that Medicare Advantage Plans are not just state but county-specific and generally limit coverage to a specified network of hospitals and doctors. Thus the level of available coverage can vary widely from location-to-location, even within the same region in a single state.

2. Uninsured Medical Expenses:

Too many retirees assume that they'll only need traditional Medicare and opt not to purchase a Medicare Supplement plan. Occasionally, some people opt out of Medicare Part B to avoid paying the premium. The common justification is that that they're healthy (now) and their relatives (who, reportedly drank and smoked heavily) all lived to ripe old ages and died in their sleep.

Unfortunately, these assumptions ignore the reality of aging; that most people will at some point in their lives, experience a major medical event which without comprehensive insurance protection, will cost far more than they realize. Adding insult to injury, these needs too often occur at the worst possible time. Fundamentally, what insurance does is replace an unknown and disproportionally large expense that can occur suddenly and without warning with a regular monthly payment that can be budgeted.

The sad fact is that most people who are under-insured or uninsured don't lack the money but rather don't want to spend their money to protect themselves from something they don't want to admit might happen. Even if they allow it might happen, they assume it will be far in the future and they'll be able to save for it (which never actually happens). But more often than not, the "it can't happen to me" denials are wrong. And despite the inevitable claim of "bad luck" and finger pointing, the real culprit is inadequate income planning. In other words, having sufficient and reliable monthly income to pay bills including insurance premiums is the easiest way to protect against financial hardship when bad things happen.

3. Long Term Care:

Based on data from the Genworth Financial research (http://newsroom.genworth.com/2015-04-09-Genworth-2015-Annual-Cost-of-Care-Study-While-Long-Term-Care-Costs-Increase-So-Does-Millennials-Confidence-in-Future-Care-Plans), Long Term Care remains the largest unfunded liability in the country. They estimate that by 2020, half the country will have at least one chronic illness and by 2030, costs will increase by 25% simply due to increasing longevity.

What's surprising to many retirees is that Medicare doesn't pay for Long Term Care. At best it (currently) only covers the first 20 days of qualified skilled nursing care, after which it pays for the next 80 days after a daily co-pay of $157.50. The daily co-pays are often covered by Medicare Supplement and Medicare Advantage plans but after 100 days, in a lifetime, there is no further coverage under Medicare.

The best solution is to have an adequate Long Term Care insurance policy but there is a cost for this. Premiums can and do vary widely based on multiple variables but as a starting point, assume an adequate insurance plan to run a few hundred dollars per month or more per person.

Good News/Bad News: Life Expectancies Are Increasing

According to the National Institute on Aging, from 2010 through 2050, there will be a 351% increase in the number of people living past 85 and 1004% increase in the number of people living past age 100. Based on their data, over the next 20 years the average life expectancy of an American will rise from about 83 to about 90.

Of course, this is both good news and bad news. In the good news category, most people in their golden years want to live longer, especially if they remain in good health. Fundamentally, what increasing longevity means is that "80 is the new 60." In the "bad news" category, increasing longevity doesn't mean the major medical needs are vanishing but rather are postponed. Unfortunately when they do occur, it's at a time of increased body frailty due to advancing age and the result is greater degrees and length of medical care and treatment to recover. That translates to greater cost.

The effect of inflation on the cost on medical treatment compounded on increasing length and complexity of treatment needed, leads to a progressive deterioration of any financial plan's margin of error safety net. It is this under-estimation of costs that contributes to plan failure. Specifically, a good retirement income plan must account for:

1. **Adequate monthly income.** This is a reliable income stream guaranteed for life that is not only adequate to pay ALL of the bills (including medical insurance premiums), but also includes a reasonable adjustment for inflation.

2. **A reserve income safety net.** This is a secondary source of income that may be triggered at any time in the event that

unforeseen circumstances cause a significant, long-term increase in the income demand, regardless of what caused that need.

3. **Emergency Fund Source.** This is a source of cash that can be tapped for emergency needs in the event that short-term or sudden large demands for cash crop up.

In all three cases, it is absolutely essential that these sources are not exposed to any risk of loss due to falling investment markets or other circumstances outside one's personal ability to control.

The Compound Effect of Taxation

Given enough taxable income, the costs of medical insurance can rise sharply. For example, a couple both 65 or older that reports an AGI of $170,000 on their tax return will pay $2,517.60 per year for Medicare Part B and no added amount for Medicare Part D. Add just $1 to the AGI, and their Medicare B and D premiums will jump to $3816 per year. That's right. $1 extra income per year cost $1298.40 in Medicare premiums. Call it unfair? Sure, but the obvious solution is report less taxable income.

Technically, there are two ways to do this. Earn less and report less. For most people, the former is not only unattractive, but it may actually be impossible. Income payments from Social Security, pensions and eventual Required Minimum Distributions (RMDs) from IRAs, etc. are always reported and once begun, cannot be stopped, even if someone wanted to. From a practical stand point that means the only solution is to report less without diminishing what is earned. Here again, there are two possible avenues: legal and illegal and nobody should give consideration to the latter. Not only are there serious and unpleasant consequences if you get caught, it's entirely unnecessary.

In 1934, Judge Learned Hand writing for the Second Circuit Court (Helvering v. Gregory, 69 F.2d 809, 810-11) famously said:

"Any one may so arrange his affairs that his taxes shall be as low as possible; he is not bound to choose that pattern which will best

pay the Treasury; there is not even a patriotic duty to increase one's taxes."

The following year that opinion was unanimously upheld by the U.S. Supreme Court (Gregory v. Helvering, 293 U.S. 465 (1935)).

Ironically, as common as Judge Hand's iconic quote about minimizing taxes is quoted, few reciters actually read the rest of what he said.

After writing that introductory remark, Judge Hand continued to say that when tax reductions are justified by individual steps which, under the strictest of literal interpretation, may seem lawful, when the aggregate otherwise produces an unlawful result (in this case, tax evasion), the entire process must be considered unlawful. This case became the landmark court decision which introduced the concept of form over function.

What we draw from this is that legal methods to reduce tax exposure are the only acceptable way, and in case you're thinking to yourself *"duhhh"* then smile knowing I'm not talking to you. But, what is about to come, must then be taken all the more seriously.

Many retirees generate unnecessary taxable income. By and large, this comes in one of two forms:

1. Generating reportable, taxable income from interest and dividend payments that are plowed back into the account and never actually spent and

2. Permitting a larger than necessary tax load on Social Security Income payments.

Dividends and Interest:

We all love growth in our investments and one of the most attractive methods of developing profit from investments is through dividend payments. Essentially, a dividend is a cash profit-sharing payment paid to shareholders annually if and when the stock company has a profitable year. Dividends are paid by individual stocks as well as by equity mutual funds (which are an aggregate of multiple individual stocks). Except in qualified plans (IRA, 401(k), 403(b), Roth IRA, etc.) dividend payments are taxable in the tax year paid whether or not they are actually received (as cash) and spent. The degree of taxability varies with multiple factors but is commonly taxed as ordinary income. The same is true of interest payments on any non-tax-deferred account.

These taxable events are reported on the income tax return (Line 8a. Taxable Interest, Line 9a. Ordinary Dividends and Line 9b. Qualified Dividends).

The sum of these taxable amounts ultimately adds to the Adjusted Gross Income (AGI) which in turn, contributes to total taxable income in three ways:

1. Directly increasing reportable income which increases AGI which

2. can increase the amount of Social Security Income that get taxed, thereby further increasing the AGI which

3. can directly reduce the amount of itemized deductions that are taken and even lead to deduction phase-outs and/or trigger Alternative Minimum Tax (which imposes a higher tax burden than otherwise).

Most surprising among these is the aspect of tax inclusion on Social Security income benefits. When first proposed by President Roosevelt in 1935, Social Security benefits were not taxed. That came later, in 1983 under President Reagan and again changed in 1993 under President Clinton. Today (2015), Social Security Income is taxable when a modified AGI calculation (18 step calculation in the 1040 instructions) exceeds certain thresholds. If half the Social Security payments plus ALL other reportable income exceeds $32,000 for a couple filing joint or $25,000 for single filers, up to half the Social Security payments are reported as taxable. But when that modified AGI calculation exceeds $44,000 for a couple or $34,000 for single, up to 85% of the Social Security benefits are taxable. In this case, "taxable" means adds to the "Bottom Line" (literally, Line 37 on Form 1040) meaning the AGI.

When the modified AGI calculation does NOT include taxable interest and dividend payments (that are otherwise not needed as income), this can have a significant effect on Social Security's taxability, including in some cases, result in NONE of a person's Social Security Income to be included in the taxable income. Not only does this increase a person's after-tax income (remember, it's not how much you make that counts, but how much you keep), it can reduce potentially reduce medical insurance premium requirements.

Required Minimum Distributions

The final insult is what happens when an IRA owner reaches the Required Beginning Age (70½) and must start liquidating his/her qualified retirement plan (IRA, 401(k), 403(b), etc.). These mandatory, fully taxable distributions can significantly increase how much Social Security benefits are taxed which yet again, compounds upon the total AGI and possible exposure to increased premium costs for medical insurance. As we've already seen, increasing AGI by just $1 can cause a significant jump in both Medicare Part B and D premiums.

But wait. There's more. Even people under age 65, who don't have Medicare insurance or even haven't started their Social Security payments still must heed these considerations. If, for example, a working couple has private medical insurance on one or both spouses, and they have qualified for health care subsidies under the Affordable Health Care Act ("Obama-Care"), the amount of reportable income can significantly impact how much subsidy they receive. Without opening the political can of worms, it's fair to say that the more a person's health care costs are subsidized (paid by someone else), the more they like the program. Love it or hate it, the U.S. Supreme Court has now twice affirmed key provisions of the Affordable Health Care Act and it's now part of our lives. Taking advantage of whatever financial benefits are available is sound financial planning and that again, returns to this notion of minimizing income tax exposure wherever possible.

QLAC

Until recently, it was impossible to avoid starting Required Minimum Distributions from qualified retirement plans at age 70½. On July 1, 2014, the U.S. Department of Treasury and I.R.S. issued a ruling which made available to average investors, the use of a Qualified Longevity Annuity Contract (QLAC). Essentially, this plan permits owners of individual IRA, 401(k), 403(b) and 457(b) plans to defer Required Minimum Distributions on the lesser of 25% of their total account or $125,000, until age 85 at which time, it is distributed according to a specified schedule. The value of this is to (potentially) significantly decrease the size of RMDs and accordingly tax load on Social Security, which in turn can reduce Adjusted Gross Income for up to 15 years.

Putting it All Together:

1. Without letting the "tax tail wag the dog," minimize exposure to taxable gains which are not actually received as income because doing so compounds onto taxable income without a corresponding spendable income benefit. Essentially this refers to non-qualified accounts (meaning not IRA, 401(k), 403(b), etc.) that are in:

    a. Large CDs, especially laddered CDs for "risk-free growth" or CDs with terms that carry from one calendar your to another.

    b. Dividend-paying investments, especially when those dividends are reinvested back into the underlying portfolio

    c. Mutual Funds with a lot of turn-over, particularly those being handled by managed account brokers.

2. When generating lifetime retirement income to supplement Social Security and Pension payments think first about using Roth IRA funds. It's what the Roth IRA was invented for. The payments received are income tax-exempt. They do not get reported on a 1040, do not add to the tax load on Social Security and do not adversely affect Medicare Insurance premiums.

3. After using Roth IRA funds, use non-IRA fixed annuities which uniquely generate income that consists of a pro-rata proportion of interest and principal and only the interest portion is taxable. Depending on circumstances, it is possible to generate lifetime for which only a fraction of the total income is taxable.

The net effect of this level of planning is to legally "arrange your affairs so your axes are as low as possible" and in doing so, minimize not only how much of your income is taxed but also minimize how much you pay for your medical insurance, both before age 65 and after.

When all is said and done, good retirement planning must account for the high and rising cost of health care, both direct (premiums) and indirect (uninsured medical expenses). Materially improving on one's overall plan may require some rethinking of the role of traditional investing.

Traditional investment planning, which is about accumulation planning, is not retirement planning which is about income. Accordingly, a sound retirement plan must regard generating permanent, lifelong income as the primary objective. At minimum, the least amount of required income is the amount necessary to pay for all reasonably anticipated expenses in retirement that is guaranteed for life. Seeking to build retirement around an unsecured and uncertain future pot of money is to invite eventual disaster. Ultimately, one measure of true personal wealth is having $1 more a month than you'll ever need or want for the rest of your life. Ironically, when it comes to health care costs, that $1 could make the difference of thousands.

Section Six:
Using Real Estate for
Retirement Income

Converting Your Dirt to Dollars: How to Take Your Real Estate and Create An Income Stream

Kyle Winkfield

Real Estate has long been favored as a top choice for many Americans' investment portfolios. Some people invest in real estate because it's what they do, it's what they love. It's more than just a means to an end, it's part of their skill set and a way they've found to contribute and enjoy life. Others invest in real estate because they see investment opportunities as a means to an end—a happy ending complete with steady stream of income. Much can be said about how real estate fares in comparison to other investment options and financial products, but if you're a real estate kind of person, you almost always identify an exit strategy with a flow of income from real estate; a way to convert the dirt into dollars and generating a paycheck from it.

So, is real estate actually a good place to invest or park your money? It's a matter of both opinion and math. A bit of luck is often involved as well, but location, timing, and most importantly, strategy are key factors. There are certain realities about real estate that the savvy investor understands, yet tend to be widely and wildly misunderstood by the masses. We will address four of them here.

Reality #1: Your real estate will appreciate or depreciate regardless of your equity position. Whether the property is owned in full or mortgaged, it will fluctuate in value based on a number of external conditions over which you have no control.

Reality #2: Your dirt earns a zero rate of return. Equity isolated by itself in the walls of a house or dirt on the ground receives no rate of return. Appreciation does not equal returns. This is a working example of the investment axiom: growth does not equal income

Reality #3: You cannot buy groceries, gas, or medicine with dirt. If you have multiple deeds but no immediate access to cash, it doesn't matter what your asset column says, you have no cash. In this case you are dirt rich yet cash poor.

Reality #4: Real estate is not a "buy and walk away" investment like most other opportunities classified as investments. Regardless of how easy the property may seem, real estate requires management, maintenance and money over your period of ownership.

Before delving into the why or how of converting dirt to dollars, you must first determine what your finish line looks like. What's the purpose of this money? Do you want to create an income stream? Begin a family legacy? Once you've decided the purpose of the money, you must pick the path to get there. This is where you weigh the benefits and drawbacks of the bevy of financial products. Do you want tax-advantaged growth on your principle? Do you want to participate in the growth of our economy and potentially outpace inflation? Do you want safety and liquidity? These are questions to start considering so as to decide the best course of action, whether you're a real estate investor, considering investment options, or a strategic homeowner.

For the purposes of approaching this from several points of view, we are going to approach real estate as a paycheck from three different angles during which we will discuss the aforementioned realities in detail:

1. For those who are considering investing in real estate, do you have other options?

2. For those who are currently real estate investors, what options do you have for turning your dirt into a paycheck?

3. For those who are not investors but own a home, what can you do to turn your home into a paycheck?

Have Money, Want to Invest

So you've accumulated some cash and feel like real estate is calling your name (maybe you've watched too much HGTV?). Perhaps you just got a real estate opportunity that you feel you can't possibly pass up. Whatever the case may be, if you are considering investing in real estate, there are many factors to consider before signing the deed. Let's revisit Reality #1:

Your real estate will appreciate or depreciate regardless of your equity position. Whether the property is owned in full or mortgaged, it will fluctuate in value based on a number of external conditions over which you have no control.

When it comes to home ownership, we've been taught that paying off our homes is priority #1. That leads to extra mortgage payments, skipped vacations, countdown clocks and a tremendous sense of pride. "I own this place free and clear." "Our house is paid for." "We don't have a mortgage." You've heard these statements before, and maybe you've also made them yourself. Home ownership is a badge of honor no matter where you live, and knowing that no one can take your roof from you, even during potential times of hardship is a big deal.

Of course when making these statements we forget that things like catastrophic illness, imminent domain, property taxes, natural disasters, and other uncontrollable scenarios can invalidate that "truth." It is possible that paying off your mortgage puts you in a more vulnerable financial position in a variety of ways including but not limited to cash on hand, taxes and estate planning.

So what do these various ruin-your-day scenarios have to do with acquiring equity in a property? It's the "own it outright" approach that we're taking to task. If owning your home "free and clear" is a very personal issue for you and nothing can dissuade you from the notion, then this approach is not for you. Put your principal where your principles are and buy the place outright. However, when it comes to strategic real estate investing, consider that there are some viable alternatives.

How about not turning all of your cash into dirt? Here's why: a property's value may appreciate. It may depreciate. A property may be earning rental income. It may sit vacant. These are details that would not change if one owed $300,000 to the bank or $0. These factors are completely independent of one another, thus we can make the statement: how much equity one has does not impact the property's investment value (or lack thereof).

Keeping with our current example, you have a $300,000 equity position in a rental property and it is earning rental income. That rent check is arriving monthly, regardless of how much you do or do not owe to the bank.

That brings us to Reality #2:

Your dirt earns a zero rate of return. Equity isolated by itself in the walls of a house or dirt on the ground receives no rate of return. Appreciation does not equal returns.

Appreciation is defined as an increase or rise in the value. Property appreciation or depreciation occurs regardless of a creditor's position in your life. Understanding that concept is key when it comes to strategic real estate investing.

Yes, your property's value may appreciate, and yes, you may be collecting rental income, but neither of these factors would be impacted whether you owe $300,000 to the bank or $0. Likewise, a property's value may depreciate. Any number of improvements (that will require additional investment) can be done to a property to increase the potential market value. Ultimately, value is determined by another uncontrollable force—the market. Other external factors to consider that impact your property's value are the perceived quality of the neighborhood, crime statistics, school quality, natural disasters and local and national economies just to name a few.

The point here is that paying off a house (often referred to as how much equity one has in a property) is not necessarily the best option, whether it be your primary residence or an investment property. Your money is at risk when it's in the dirt and you don't control many of the factors that will determine its value when you are ready to sell. The investment is not earning you any additional money from its reallocation from your bank account to your dirt. You could be utilizing the beauty of leverage to kill two birds with one stone. Always be aware of the opportunity cost of dedicating cash to any real estate venture. If you mortgaged the property and put your cash into a relatively safe interest-bearing liquid investment, instead of into the dirt, would you come out ahead once all is said and done?

Have Dirt, Need Money

Reality #3:

You cannot buy groceries, gas, or medicine with dirt. If you have multiple deeds but no immediate access to cash, it doesn't matter what your asset column says. You have no cash.

At this juncture in the discussion, some might say "Well, when I need money I'll just sell a property. That's the plan." This sounds great in theory, but in addition to the effort and expenses involved in selling property, that plan is missing some key details:

There is a serious laundry list of external factors impacting the conversion of dirt to dollars:

- The state of the real estate market as a whole, which impacts your buyer pool and overall property values

- Current interest rates

- Appraisal values and area comps

- Neighborhood statistics and demographics

- Area crime statistics

- Neighborhood school quality and ratings

- Weather and natural disasters (think your zip code isn't at risk? consider Hurricane Sandy)

- Local and national economies (to include unemployment rates)

- Property taxes

- Future tax rates

- Capital gains costs

- New developments (that may be an improvement to your area, but present competition in the form of newer properties that compete with yours)

- government plans and interventions (not to be limited to imminent domain, changes in code, seizures, future highway plans, etc.)

- current tenants (they can be great or make your life a nightmare)

- As well, there are myriad personal factors impacting the conversion of dirt to dollars:

- Catastrophic illness (yourself or a loved one who needs your care/time/financial support)

- General health (perhaps you are not in imminent danger but your health is impacted enough that your ability to properly manage your property is compromised)

- Disability

- Dependents (dependent care, whether it be that of a spouse, parent, child or grandchild can inhibit your ability to be a property manager)

- Job change (if you're burning the candle at both ends, maintaining a job and your real estate portfolio, what happens if your company relocates you?)

- Stress (a factor that impacts health, but a big enough deal that it deserves its own bullet point)

- Additional factors impacting the conversion of dirt to dollars:

- Negative equity ("upside down" in the mortgage)

- Complicated ownership situation (perhaps more than one person or entity is involved)

- Costs associated with property sales (commissions, appraisals, settlement costs, repairs, etc.)

While your plan may be to manage your properties and sell them off when your budget requires, there are a lot of unforeseeable and uncontrollable factors at play that are going to affect your performance. If you have yet to invest in real estate, but are considering doing so, consider these factors before jumping in. If you are already investing in real estate, review these issues and be certain that you are not putting too many eggs in a dirt basket without having weighed all the options. At the end of the day, you cannot break off a shingle and trade it for your medicine at the corner pharmacy. Being real estate rich and cash poor does not pay the bills or make dinner. If you have investment property and want to turn it into a paycheck that will keep the lights on and bread in the oven, keep reading.

Let's return to our initial example of your $300,000 property. Remember when we mentioned the downside of "free and clear" ownership, the transition of cash to dirt? Now is a good time to take a closer look at that scenario. If you own the property outright, whether it was a cash purchase or you worked hard to pay off the mortgage, you now have a substantially large amount of money buried in the ground. Sure, you can sell it, but considering the uncontrollable factors listed above, there are obviously a lot of circumstances that impact the sale, not to mention the length of time it can take. If an emergency arises, you typically can't sell your property overnight (know any rich drug lords who owe you a favor?), and even if you consider another option such as running to the bank, loans and refinancing, it won't solve your problems immediately either. You don't have control over whether a bank will grant you the privilege of turning your dirt into cash, nor how long it may take to complete that transaction. Even if you are relatively successful in converting property as financial needs arise, you've lost money during the process that could've been earning elsewhere, and if you've got more than one investment property, you're still doing the property management grind. So now that we've established that you can't buy medicine with a shingle, let's talk about replacing that shingle using Reality #4:

> *Real estate is not a "buy and walk away" investment like most other opportunities classified as investments. Regardless of how easy the property may seem, real estate requires management, maintenance and money over your period of ownership.*

Perhaps part of your retirement plan was to create a second career—property management. You might have visions of Donald Trump or an HGTV star when this plan came to mind, but you should probably look more towards the property management office that runs your neighborhood HOA. Property management is not easy or glamorous. It should not be written off as something to "keep me busy" in retirement, unless of course, you enjoy 3am phone calls from tenants who have a ruptured pipe or broken HVAC. Some people really do enjoy that, and if you're one of them, then party on. For most people, broken pipes and non-functioning HVAC units, new roof estimates and tenant-landlord court don't sound like the definition of retirement, and it certainly doesn't sound like why people buy investment real estate in the first place.

Most real estate investors will explain that they own multiple investment properties so that they can use the rental income as a consistent income stream. That's another theory that sounds great, but when put to the test has some challenges. In addition to the aforementioned bulleted list of things that can get in the way of selling a property, consider that many of the items on those lists can also impact the management and maintenance of a property. Catastrophic illness, death, and disability are just a few factors that could "get in the way" of managing your properties.

You could be walking down the street one afternoon and severely disabled the next. Your properties would still need attention, management and maintenance. Depending on the severity of your personal situation, you might need to use the rental income to address your medical bills. It might also be the time that a new roof needs to be installed on property A, and you've just lost your tenant at property B, so you've lost part of your income. If an uncontrollable event occurs in your life, how would you be able to manage your situation?

Even if you've covered a lot of your bases in the "unforeseen" arena with long term care insurance or some extra money set aside, you still have the property management burden for as long as you own the property. We often hear, "My tenant paid my mortgage for me for 30 years, now the rent is all mine! That's my income!" But to maintain that cash flow, you're forgetting all of the maintenance that is required to assure that the flow of cash continues unimpeded. The only thing guaranteed about real estate is maintenance. Consider the expenses involved in maintaining real estate income over a certain period of time: heat pumps, HVAC, new roofs, new appliances, landscaping, paint and carpet (after each tenant), new windows, pavement resurfacing, general repairs, septic repairs/replacement, pest control, HOA/Condo fees, property taxes, insurance, and special assessment fees. That's a short list and we also have to consider the uncertainty of other human beings. When you're going this route, you are counting on another human being to create your paycheck. Retirement is all about freedom—when you're supposed to be financially independent and do things your way…but if your properties are your income, you're going to be chained to the mailbox hoping that your tenant keeps up their end of the deal.

Using real estate to create a paycheck in retirement can be an iffy proposition. There are substantial risks to the safety and liquidity of your investment, and you should consider if risking your savings is even necessary. For most people approaching retirement, you are running out of time, and turning your cash into dirt is no different than taking your savings to Vegas. It can be a good fit for the right people, with the right temperament and resources, but be aware if you are considering real estate as your primary retirement income-producing asset, there can be significant headwinds to turning dirt into actual cash.

Have 5 Bedrooms, Only Need 3?

One last angle to consider is that of the non-investor who is looking at their home thinking "what now?" You've spent time and money building a life in a home that now might be in a neighborhood, climate, state, or country in which you no longer want or need to be. If you've followed the traditional approach of paying off your home, you might be considering options for retirement and thinking about those dollars in your dirt. There are options on the table, some of which include reverse mortgages, home equity loans and downsizing. All viable options, and if you don't need 5 bedrooms, why have them? If you've built up a considerable amount of equity in your home or have paid it off, why not consider those options for turning your home back into dollars.

Dirt to Dollar Options

As a real estate investor facing retirement decisions, there are three main approaches:

1. Turn it into your retirement job, otherwise known as property management.

2. Continue management and sell an investment as income is needed.

3. Convert your dirt to dollars.

We've thoroughly discussed why the first two options can be less desirable, so let's investigate a third approach which involves strategically transitioning your dirt to dollars. We've addressed how equity in a property has no bearing on its investment potential; owning it "outright" or owing the bank does not impact whether or not you can generate rental income. As such, why have your cash buried in the ground when it could be positioned elsewhere, also earning income? If you love your properties and want to retain them, at least consider making your *dirt and* your dollars work for you at the same time.

When it comes to turning your dirt into retirement dollars, you can create a guaranteed income stream whether you plan to be a property manager or you want to cash out. Whichever route you take, there are several financial products that can generate a healthy, safe and consistent rate of return on your cash without subjecting it to market risk. Make sure that when establishing your guaranteed income stream, you have an account in place that meets the following criteria:

- Tax-Deferred Growth: money grows unencumbered by taxes

- Tax-Free Distributions: money withdrawn from the account is not subject to income tax

- Compound Interest: uninterrupted compound interest is the 8th world wonder

- Competitive Rate of Return: any rate of return is better than the 0% from your dirt

- High Contribution Limits: when you're cashing out of real estate, investment accounts with low contribution caps aren't helpful

- Liquidity: you can access your cash without having to ask the bank, refinance, sell the property, etc.

- No-Loss Provision: your principle is safeguarded and any gains are locked in annually; you cannot lose your money

As a homeowner, there are three main approaches to accessing dollars through your home:

1. Reverse mortgage,

2. home equity line of credit / refinance, or

3. sell your home, get a cheaper one, and convert those leftover dollars into a paycheck.

Now keep in mind, that home equity loans and reverse mortgages should never be used for market-risk investment purposes (you could lose the money and then what?!) but if you want to utilize these options to get liquidity from your equity, they are certainly viable options. Both of these approaches are for people who want to remain in their home but also want access to their equity.

Reverse mortgages take part of the equity in your home and convert it into payments to you; an advanced payment on your home equity. The money you get is usually tax-free and generally you don't have to pay back the money for as long as you live in your home. When you die, sell your home or move out, you, your spouse or your estate must repay the loan. What's risky about this approach is that you get a set amount of money and that's it—if you spend through the cash, it's gone.

A home equity line of credit is an ability to access a portion of your equity, as the bank will grant this credit line based on a percentage of your home equity position. This is an option for obtaining more liquidity, but it doesn't really turn your dirt to dollars. Keep in mind that during the financial crisis of 2008 that banks were reducing and freezing homeowner's lines of credit; you might have a line of credit, but you don't have control.

You might consider the third option—selling your home and moving into a cheaper one where you can capture some of those equity dollars. What then? Just like a real estate investor considering what to do with the proceeds of a real estate deal, seek financial products that can generate a healthy, safe and consistent rate of return on your cash without subjecting it to market risk.

Here is a scorecard of the various financial products available on the market that can be used for investment or income-generating purposes once you've converted your dirt to dollars.

	High Cash Value Permanent Life Insurance	Qualified Plan (401k, IRA)	Stocks/Mutual Funds	Real Estate Investment Trust (REIT)	Muni Bonds	Bonds	Business	CD	Money Market	Annuity
Safe Harbor	Y	Y	N	N	N	N	N	N	N	Y
Guaranteed Growth	Y*	N	N	N	N	N	N	Y	N	Y*
Tax-Deferred Accumulation	Y	Y	N	N	N	N	N	N	N	Y
Tax-Free Use	Y	N	N	N	Y	N	N	N	N	N
Competitive Rate of Return	Y*	Y*	Y*	Y*	N	Y*	Y*	N	N	Y*
Guaranteed Income Stream	N	N	N	N	N	N	N	N	N	Y
No-Loss Provisions	Y	N	N	N	N	N	N	Y	Y	Y*
Liquidity, Use & Control	Y	D	Y	D	D	D	N	N	Y	Y*
High Contribution Limits	Y	N	Y	Y	Y	Y	Y	Y	Y	Y
Collateral	Y	N	N	N	N	N	D	Y	N	N
Additional Benefits	Y	N	N	N	N	N	D	N	N	Y

Here is the Bottom Line. If you are facing retirement, it's time to make your money safe. You've spent a lot of time, effort and energy developing your nest egg and now is not the time to put it at further risk. If you own investment real estate and want a predictable income stream for retirement, seek a safe and secure compounded growth account that is guaranteed on a tax-advantaged basis where your neither your principle nor your prior gains are at risk. Regardless of what phase of life you're in, it's never too early or too late to establish a predictable income stream for retirement. There are several financial products that can accomplish this and won't wake you up at 3AM to tell you that the air conditioning is out.

At the end of the day, if real estate makes your heart happy, as long as you can afford your life, then by all means go buy that property. However, if you're looking at real estate as a means to achieve your primary source of retirement income, please be certain to consider all of the factors discussed here and consult a retirement income specialist. He's not likely to be calling you at 3am with a busted water pipe.

What's the Deal with the NEW Reverse Mortgage?

By Shelley Giordano,
Author, "What's the Deal with Reverse Mortgages?"

I f you are like me, you may cringe when yet another celebrity spokes-person pops up on your television touting a reverse mortgage. Try as I might, I can't get past the aura of irresponsible lending that encouraged folks to tap home equity in the go-go years of the Housing Bubble of the last decade. This is unfortunate because there is growing body of academic work, supported by esteemed thought leaders, who are demonstrating that a reverse mortgage can provide truly significant safeguards for other assets. You may be surprised by this notion, as was I, but it is true: using a reverse mortgage in a deliberative manner designed to protect one's overall wealth is the new zeitgeist in retirement income planning.

Make no mistake about it, this new approach is possible only because HUD/FHA has acted to rectify program design in the original Home Equity Conversion Mortgage, which is the most common "reverse mortgage." Today, homeowners without the means or willingness to keep current on homeowner obligations, such as tax and insurance, may not participate in a HECM. Homeowners also are prevented from using "too much too soon"[30] of their reverse mortgage so that there are funds available later in retirement. Younger spouses who would have been

---

30 Wade Pfau, PhD, CFA, Professor Retirement Income The American College, Private Correspondence

displaced in the past when the primary borrower died are protected. And finally, changes in how the program is structured and sold on the secondary market allow the homeowner to "negotiate down" upfront acquisition costs if they prefer taking a higher interest rate, just like any other mortgage. It is actually possible to start off a reverse mortgage with a loan balance as little as $125 with some lenders!

Actually the HECM program has always enjoyed significant consumer safeguards. These can be summed up in what I call, the Four Nevers©.[31] Provided clients meet their homeowner obligations such as taxes, insurance and routine maintenance:

- The homeowner and his estate never give up the title to the home.

- The homeowner, when leaving the house, or his estate, can never owe more than the home's value; conversely, when the house is sold, sale proceeds in excess of the debt amount belong to the borrower /estate.

- Even if all the money that can be borrowed through the reverse mortgage has reached its limit, the homeowner never has to move.

- Monthly repayments are never required or expected, although voluntary payments are accepted.

Financial advisers and their clients immediately comprehend the wisdom of diversifying assets. It's as easy as remembering what you learned in kindergarten: Don't keep all your eggs in one basket. Yet, investigators have noted that the housing asset represents an enormous **undiversified** asset. Owners tend to treat the house as a "sacred cow" even though its value is solely dependent on the local housing market.

By electing to use the asset for other purposes, even if only to initiate a HECM Standby Line of Credit, owners can convert the asset to an insurance policy, for example, or substitute it for taxable income. In doing so, benefits not normally associated with housing wealth may improve the

---

31 The 4 Nevers © 2000, Shelley Giordano

homeowner's overall financial security. And this improvement is realized without any loss of the shelter and enjoyment of the home.

The HECM Line of Credit

Few advisers are aware that a HECM reverse mortgage can be structured as a growing Line of Credit (LOC). The Line of Credit grows in borrowing capacity at a *contractually dictated* rate, meaning that the LOC grows regardless of what housing values are in your neighborhood when you want to monetize your home investment by either selling, or drawing on your reverse mortgage.[32] Again, researchers have recognized that placing a HECM LOC on your home allows:

1. A hedge against declining home values.

2. A possible hedge against inflation as the LOC grows at the prevailing interest rate.

3. A revolving LOC in which voluntary payments on loan balance "reappear" as available credit in the LOC column.

4. Unlike a traditional Home Equity Line of Credit, the HECM LOC cannot be frozen, cancelled, or reduced.

The HECM as a Standby Antidote to Market Volatility

By far, the most significant finding is the HECM's ability to substitute for portfolio draws in bear markets. Advisers are wary of "sequence of returns risk" and reverse dollar cost averaging, which just means having to sell increasing numbers of shares to meet spending needs when the market is down. We know this as "buy low, sell high" and by all means, everybody knows they should AVOID selling low. Study after study demonstrates that draws from a reverse mortgage during market declines not only help protect the portfolio but also can contribute to overall residual wealth for legacy purposes.[33]

---

32 This rate is the monthly applicable interest rate +1/12 the MIP of 1.25%.

33 *https://www2.bc.edu/~sunwc/paper/RM.pdf*

Tax Equivalents

There is growing interest in the HECM by portfolio theorists and other academicians, in part because of tax considerations. When a client borrows money from his house via a Home Equity Line of Credit (HELOC), the draws from that loan are not treated as income for tax purposes. Likewise, proceeds from a HECM loan are not treated as income for tax purposes.

Therefore, drawing from the HECM LOC may have tax advantages over other forms of cash flow during retirement.

In the *Journal of Financial Planning*, Gerald Wagner, PhD, noted in his paper *The 6% Solution*:

> *"For example, a 63-year-old borrower with $250,000 available for a payment plan could receive $1,449 each month from a HECM tenure plan; that is $17,387 per year, and because these are nontaxable loan advances, the payment's tax equivalent value is considerably higher. If the marginal federal bracket was 28.0%, and the borrower lived in California (10.3 % tax rate), the tax equivalent value of these tenure advances would be $26,740."[34]*

For this client, drawing home equity at the rate of $17,387 is the equivalent of having drawn $26,740 from his portfolio. Thomas C. B. Davison, MA, PhD, CFP®, discovered the same tax advantage in using home equity when compared to portfolio draws (private correspondence):

> *"The way to figure out what you can spend is first to figure out what the tax is, then subtract that from the withdrawal, and spend what's left. If the tax rate is 33%, then the tax on $1.50 is $1.50 x 0.33, which is $0.49.5, leaving you $1.00 to spend after a bit of rounding. Or in fractions: the tax is (1/3) x $1.50 = $1.50/3, or 50 cents."[35]*

For every dollar spent in home equity, that's $1.50 not withdrawn from the portfolio.

---

34 *https://www.onefpa.org/journal/Pages/The%206.0%20Percent%20Rule.aspx*
35 *From private correspondence*

Tax Bracket Creep

Others have noted that substituting draws from a reverse mortgage to avoid large draws from other assets may prevent triggering a higher tax rate. For example, Wade D. Pfau, PhD, CFA, Professor of Retirement Income, The American College wrote: *"Proceeds from a reverse mortgage or from the cash value of life insurance could also be used in such a way to boost spending without increasing taxable income."2*[36]

Understanding How Interest Payments on HECM Loans Can Be Deducted

People who plan to use their HECM as a revolving line of credit want to know how payments on the loan balance can qualify for mortgage interest deductions. Of course, mortgage interest is only deductible when paid. Reverse mortgages are treated the same way as traditional forward mortgages; mortgage interest is deductible, but only when paid, not just accrued. Because the HECM loan balance increases at not only the interest rate but the MIP rate as well, care must be taken to determine how much of the total amount owed is interest and hence can be deducted:

- The ongoing 1.25% Mortgage Insurance Premium (MIP) is not considered interest, although it is part of the compounding rate. The interest charge is the sum of the variable component (LIBOR) and the lender's margin.

- If the borrower does not make payments on mortgage until the loan ends, all the interest will be paid off as a lump sum, resulting in a large deduction in one year. The deduction may be larger than the taxable income in that year! It may be on the estate tax return if the home is sold and mortgage paid off after death.

- As the monthly addition to the loan balance is both MIP and interest, not all of it will be deductible.

    ¤ "If you currently have a HECM reverse mortgage, then your payments are applied in the following order: first to that

36 *http://blogs.wsj.com/experts/2015/03/19/how-to-increase-your-after-tax-wealth-in-retirement/*

part of your loan balance representing mortgage insurance premiums, secondly to that part of your loan balance representing servicing fees, thirdly to that part of your loan balance representing interest charges, and finally to that part of your loan balance representing principal advances. The National Reverse Mortgage Lenders Association strongly advises that you confirm with your loan servicer the manner in which your partial prepayments will be applied to your specific account." (NRMLA, 2014)[37]

- ¤ A payment will at most be partially deductible. Any payment less than the currently accumulated MIP and servicing fees would not be deductible. Note that the interest component of the monthly compounding rate will be larger than the MIP and servicing fees—typically a much larger fraction, especially as interest rates rise.

- ¤ In the Standby Reverse Mortgage scenario used by Salter et al.,[38] all the money borrowed in market downturns was paid back when markets recovered, so all the interest paid during that market downturn would be deductible.[39]

The Lost Tax Deduction for Estate Planning

As a result of a conversation with loan officer Nick Maningas of Philadelphia, Dr. Barry H. Sacks investigated the effect of taking a deduction of the accumulated interest from a reverse mortgage to offset the income tax due from the borrower's heir(s) following the borrower's death:

The use of the reverse mortgage results in accrued interest. Because the interest is accrued, but is not actually paid, by the borrower, the borrower does not have an income tax deduction for that interest. The interest deduction seems to be "lost". However, that deduction

37 *https://www.nrmlaonline.org/*

38 *https://www.onefpa.org/journal/pages/may14-hecm-reverse-mortgages-now-or-last-resort.aspx*

39 Thomas C. B. Davison, MA, PhD, CFP®, *www.toolsforretirementplanning.com*

can be recovered by the borrower's beneficiary (or beneficiaries) in the following way: 401(k) accounts and rollover IRAs are among the few assets, that, when left to beneficiaries, subject the beneficiaries to income tax. Some or all of that income tax can be eliminated by the use of the following simple technique (by which the beneficiary gets an interest deduction to offset some or all of the income from the rollover IRA or 401(k) account): Be sure that the decedent's home, which is subject to the reverse mortgage debt, goes <u>directly</u> to the same heir (or heirs) who is (or are) the beneficiary (or beneficiaries) of the decedent's 401(k) account or rollover IRA, <u>and</u> be sure that the home becomes a "qualified residence" (as defined in the Internal Revenue Code) of the heir (or heirs) <u>before</u> it is sold. (The conventional approach to dealing with the assets would be to have the estate sell the home and distribute the proceeds. The approach described is different from the conventional approach, and may need to be written into the client's will or trust.)[40]

Tax-Free Way to Fund Other Financial Products?

There are no restrictions on how HECM funds are used. For instance, it's possible to use tax-free HECM draws to fund existing insurance policies, or create new ones. Beneficiaries, of course, receive life insurance proceeds tax-free.

Some advisers view the compounding growth in the HECM Line of Credit as a way of self insuring for long term care. If the long term care expense never materializes, the client has lost nothing by setting up the fund but has hedged against the possibility that future health care needs could otherwise drain assets.

As a caution, clients considering using housing wealth to purchase Long Term Care Insurance, however, are advised to make sure that the policy premiums can be sustained until the care is needed. In *Falling Short: The Coming Retirement Crisis*, authors Charles D. Ellis, Alicia H. Munnell, and Andrew D. Eschtruth, note that they

---

40 *Private correspondence with author*

"...strongly favor a catastrophic policy with premiums paid up front. This product would pay for benefits only after the individual has paid, for say, 12 months of nursing home care, or $80,000. This arrangement would change an unbounded black hole of expense into a known quantity. Moreover, the premium for this benefit would be relatively modest and could be paid in single lump sum at retirement so buyers need not worry about premium costs climbing as they age. The hope would be that once people understood the dimensions for their exposure to long-term care costs, they would feel more comfortable about spending their balances and tapping their home equity. Unfortunately, such a product does not currently exist in the United States."

Roth Conversion Taxes

If the portfolio must be tapped to pay taxes on a Roth IRA conversion, some advisers suggest using a draw from a reverse mortgage to cover the tax bite. The advantage of this approach is that it uses untaxed money to pay the tax on the conversion. Using money from the traditional IRA itself would reduce the remaining IRA amount. For example, if the taxpayer is in the 30% tax bracket, and converts a $100,000 traditional IRA, paying the tax with money from the IRA, the remaining IRA amount, in the Roth IRA, will be $70,000. If, instead, the taxpayer uses a reverse mortgage credit line draw to pay the tax, there will be $100,000 in the Roth IRA. Growth in a Roth IRA is not taxable.

Deferring Social Security Using the HECM as an Income Bridge

The media continue to highlight strategies on to how maximize social security benefits. Many people would like to defer taking benefits until age 70 because of the substantial increase in benefits earned with that delay.[41] The chart below demonstrates that a delay in taking benefits results in a much higher monthly payment.

---

41 For an overview of social security claiming strategies, see Mary Beth Franklin at: *http://www.investmentnews.com/section/retirement2*

Chart 1

Social Security Benefits by Age

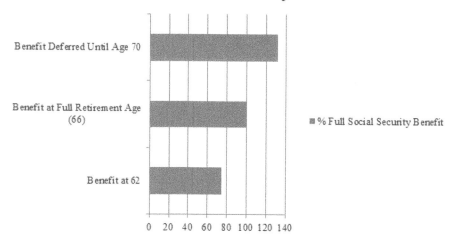

The problem with waiting until age 70 is giving up income in those years from 62-70 until qualifying for the maximum payout at 70. Thomas C. B. Davison, MA, PhD, CFP® published a case study on his blog, *www. toolsforretirementplanning.com*, in which the client uses home equity for income during many of the deferral years. The survival probability for the client's plan improved from 5% to 90%. This case illustrates how a homeowner could use a reverse mortgage to fund her needs for the first 6 years. Once the HECM funds are exhausted, she relies on her portfolio. But at age 70, she is able to reduce her portfolio draws because she is getting the largest possible social security benefit. Interestingly, the reasons her plan showed such improvement in financial stability are not just related to getting a higher social security benefit at 70:

- This client's reverse mortgage funded 6+ years of spending.
- She had more assets to spend because she added $240,000 in home wealth to her $500,000 IRA.
- Taxes matter: This client was in the 33%+ tax bracket, State/Federal combined. The Reverse Mortgage was tax-free so every $1.00 draw has the spending power of $1.50 drawn from the

IRA. In total, the $240,000 spent from her Reverse Mortgage was the equivalent of $360,000 of IRA funds.

- The investment portfolio was untouched for an extra 6 years. Keeping the portfolio invested reduces chances that she will encounter a bad sequence of returns early in retirement.

- At age 70, she enjoys the highest Social Security benefits possible, further reducing portfolio draws in her later years.

Chart 2

Portfolio Comparison Using HECM to Fund Deferral Years

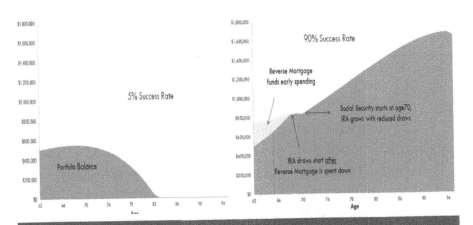

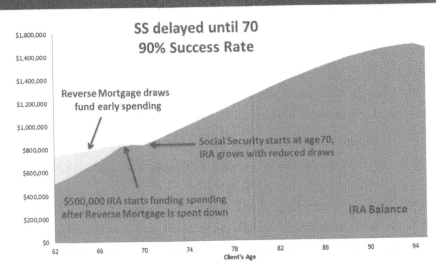

Dr. Jack Guttentag is a Professor Emeritus at the University of Pennsylvania Wharton School of Business and has been a vocal HECM proponent for years on his web site.[42] Never one to mince words, Dr. Guttentag states:

"The HECM reverse mortgage is one of the best engineered financial tools of our generation, designed to meet a wide spectrum of senior needs, from repairing the roof of their home, to paying for their grandchildren's education, to meeting expected and unexpected contingencies. Yet the program elicits negative reactions from large segments of the media, whose distorted descriptions of the HECM program are scaring off millions of seniors whose lives could be enriched by it."

He recommends that retirees establish a HECM Line of Credit early enough to enjoy compounding growth for many years:

"The use of the HECM reverse mortgage program as a type of insurance policy employs the credit line feature of the program. The senior uses her borrowing power to draw the largest line available, and lets the line sit unused until she needs it. The longer the senior lives, the longer the credit line sits unused, and the larger it becomes. While her financial assets are gradually being depleted, her credit line is getting larger. She draws on the line if she needs the money, otherwise the equity in her house will pass to her estate.

*Why the urgency? The size of the initial HECM credit lines that can be drawn are inversely related to interest rates, while the growth rate of existing unused lines is directly related to rates. Hence, a senior with a specified amount of equity gets the **maximum insurance coverage by taking out the HECM while interest rates are still low, and letting it sit unused as rates rise in the future."***

The HECM as a Hedge Against Declining Home Values

Wade D. Pfau, PhD, CFA, Professor of Retirement Income, The American College of Financial Services, published an article in *Advisor Perspectives*

---

42 *www.mtgprofessor.com*

demonstrating that establishing a HECM Line of Credit early provides a hedge against home values dropping:

> *"With the current HECM rules, those living in their homes long enough could reap a large windfall when the line of credit exceeds the home's value. This potential windfall is amplified by today's low interest rates. Even if the value of the home declines, the line of credit will continue to grow without regard for the home's subsequent value. Combining this with the fact that a HECM is a non-recourse loan means that the HECM provides a very valuable hedging property for home prices."*[43]

Conclusion

The notion that the house should never be used to fund retirement except in the most dire circumstances is dying. The "last resort strategy" was never subjected to any thoughtful and quantitative analysis, and the financial world just blindly accepted that a reverse mortgage "should" only be used when all other assets were exhausted. When this approach was subjected to the bright light of mathematics, it became clear that there was no reason to continue advocating a "wait and pray" approach. This is especially true now that academicians fully understand how the HECM Line of Credit compounds over the course of retirement. In fact, the retiree can be in danger of missing out on the compounding value a HECM LOC provides. More abstractly, setting up a HECM LOC early in retirement helps the retiree reserve the right to use his equity, *if he wants to*, later in retirement. Today's lower acquisition costs, great consumer safeguards, and careful research are strong motivators to giving serious thought to how the prudent, conservative use of the housing asset can help Americans achieve greater retirement income security. Recent research treats the HECM as an alternative asset that can be used in concert with other sources of income, often with a synergistic effect.

---

43 *http://www.advisorperspectives.com/newsletters14/Hidden_Value_of_Reverse_ Mortgage_Standby_Line_of_Credit.php*

About the Contributors

MICHAEL FOGUTH

Michael Foguth, Founder of Foguth Financial Group, specializes in working with retirees and those nearing retirement who desire to protect their hard earned money and ensure that it is there when they need it. Michael has become one of the national premier experts when it comes to retirement planning in today's economic times. His first book titled "Successonomics" was released in September of 2014; the book was Co-Authored with Steve Forbes. Within its first week it was on 5 different Amazon best sellers list, the book also awarded Michael an induction into the National Academy of Best Sellers. Michael has also been featured in local and nation publications such as; ABC, NBC, FOX, Wall Street Journal, Forbes, and USA Today. For more information please visit foguthfinancial.com or call 844-4-FOGUTH.

SHELLEY GIORDANO

Shelley Giordano is principal at the consulting firm Longevity View Associates in Washington, DC. Her firm provides reverse mortgage expertise to financial institutions. In addition, she is Co-Founder and Chair of the Funding Longevity Task Force. In this role she leads a group of academicians whose research demonstrates that the prudent use of housing wealth throughout retirement conveys significant cash flow security. She is the author of *What's the Deal with Reverse Mortgages?* and advocates for financial literacy with Women in Housing and Finance. She is a member of the FPA and NAIFA.

WILL HEIL

Will Heil has over twenty five years of professional experience in accounting and finance. He received his Certified Public Accounting license in 1995, earned the Personal Financial Specialist designation from the American Institute of Certified Public Accountants in 2008 and his CERTIFIED FINANCIAL PLANNER TM certification in 2009. Prior to entering the financial services field in 2005, Will was an accountant for public companies in the energy and telecommunications industries for eight years. Before that he worked for owner-operated businesses in engineering and automobile services. Will's career began in public accounting after graduating from Penn State in 1987 with a Bachelor of Science degree in accounting. A native of central Pennsylvania, Will has spent most of his career in Maryland and has lived in Severn with his two daughters since 1996. Will is a member of the American Institute of Certified Public Accountants and the Maryland Association of Certified Public Accountants. He has served as treasurer of non-profit organizations, including the Northern Anne Arundel County Chamber of Commerce and AT:LAST, Inc., The Maryland Assistive Technology Cooperative.

JEFF KLAUENBERG

Jeff Klauenberg, MA, CIS, CFP and owner of Klauenberg Retirement Solutions, began his Wealth Management career in 1983. His firm has continually aimed to be on the "cutting edge" of financial and retirement planning.Focusing on the retirement years, the firm provides a wide-range of retirement, investment, and tax advisory services that unify all aspects of the individual's retirement life. Through the 1980's, Mr. Klauenberg was an active member of the International Association of Financial Planning. In 1997-1998 he was a Board member of the Financial Planning Association's National Chapter helping promote the growth of Financial Planning. He was named by Baltimore Magazine to the 2011 Five Star Wealth Managers list which represents less than five percent of the wealth managers in the Baltimore area. In May 2014, Klauenberg Retirement Solutions was one of twenty wealth management firms selected by Forbes

Magazine to be highlighted in their Capital Region Financial Leaders section. Jeff and his wife, Sue, have five children and five grandchildren. They have lived in Laurel for over 30 years and have been actively involved in school activities and volunteered as various commissioners with the Laurel Boy's and Girl's Club. To contact Jeff, please call 301-317-0401 or visit www.klauenbergretirementsolutions.com.

JIM MERKLINGHAUS

Jim Merklinghaus of JM & KM Wealth Management ranks among the most highly-qualified insurance and financial professionals in the New Jersey/ New York metropolitan area. With almost 30 years of experience, Jim helps individuals and institutions by providing solid answers, practical solutions and tailored advice. Jim can be contacted at JM & KM Wealth Management at (201) 723-4926.

KYLE O'DELL

Kyle O'Dell, managing partner at O'Dell, Winkfield, Roseman & Shipp, has been crafting financial strategies to meet the complex needs of families and medical professionals for more than 20 years. As a Fiduciary for his clients, Kyle brings to the firm a passion for solving problems, and deep understanding of the demanding lives of his clientele. Kyle is an Investment Advisor, and is also life insurance licensed. To contact Kyle, please call 877-821-OWRS (6977) or visit www.owrsfirm.com.

JACK TATAR

Jack Tatar is author of "Having the Talk" and "Retire Safely: The Four Keys to a Safe Retirement". Jack is owner of GEM Research Solutions, a leading market research company specializing in the financial services industry. Jack is currently a contributor on Marketwatch.com as one of their RetireMentors. Jack is also the Bitcoin expert on About.com and co-author of "What's the Deal with Bitcoin?" Jack can be reached at Jack@Safe4Retirement.com and on his website at www.Safe4Retirement.com.

MICHAEL TOVE

Michael Tove Ph.D., CEP, RFC, president and founder of AIN Services, is an insurance licensed Certified Estate Planner (member National Institute of Certified Estate Planners) and Registered Financial Consultant (member International Association of Registered Financial Consultants). A published author and guest speaker on syndicated radio programs regarding finance, he works with clients at all levels of financial, estate and insurance planning. Dr. Tove's philosophy is that every client, regardless of net worth, deserves the best planning that can be had. Over the years, he has developed a substantial network of professionals to which he can refer if clients' specific needs are in areas other than his personal expertise. In addition, he is privileged to be a member of the elite organization, The Independent Excellence Group, a national think tank organization composed top wealth management and planning professionals to stay at the cutting edge of wealth management and financial planning solutions tailored for the most affluent and demanding individuals in the country. For more information please call 800-363-2296.

KYLE WINKFIELD

Kyle Winkfield, managing partner at O'Dell, Winkfield, Roseman & Shipp, has more than 15 years of experience growing clients' wealth through cutting edge financial strategies. Kyle specifically focuses on reducing or eliminating future income tax liabilities and preservation of wealth while increasing lifestyle security. To contact Kyle, please call 877-821-OWRS (6977) or visit www.owrsfirm.com.